SMART

with Dr. Sood

The Four-Module Stress
Management And Resiliency
Training Program

Amit Sood, M.D. M.S. F.A.C.P.

ISBN 13: 978-0-9995525-4-4
ISBN 10: 0-9995525-4-6
Library of Congress Control Number: 2019937136
LCCN Imprint Name: Global Center for Resiliency and Wellbeing, Rochester, MN

Disclaimer

The information in this book is not intended to substitute a physician's advice or medical care. Please consult your physician or other health care provider if you are experiencing any symptoms or have questions pertaining to the information contained in this book.

Most human brains have to lift an excessive cognitive and emotional load that they are ill-equipped to carry.

Our brains struggle with focus, fatigue and fear, that limit our ability to lift the life's load.

Decreasing the load is an obvious, but often a difficult-to-implement solution.

Enhancing our brain's capacity to lift the load is a low-hanging fruit worth exploring.

The SMART program helps you understand your brain's vulnerabilities, develop an intentional, focused and sustained attention, and a resilient mindset.

Together, the insights and practices of the SMART program help you create a resilient brain, that is essential to a fulfilling and productive life.

The program is being used by individuals to improve their health and wellbeing, relationships and productivity, and by organizations to foster a culture of resilience and wellbeing.

To my patients and colleagues. You have taught me so much and with such humility and grace. I will forever be grateful to you. I admire your resilience.

Dear friend,

Thank you for trusting me with your time.

SMART, in one short volume, provides you with the basis as well as the skills of the stress management and resiliency training (SMART) program. It is written as a straightforward, actionable manuscript, focusing on brevity and clarity, that presents the gist of what I have learned in my thirty-years journey to understand and help the human condition.

I have written a few books now on stress management, resilience, mindfulness, and happiness. You will likely find some of the ideas written in my other books repeated here, albeit in a new language. That repetition is purposeful to offer the core SMART approach in one volume.

The essence of the SMART approach is summarized in the accompanying figure. The program has four modules (Gratitude, Mindful Presence, Kindness, and Resilient Mindset), and three core content areas (Awareness, Attention, and Attitude).

Each insight and practice of *SMART* will help you unpack this essence, so you can effortlessly embody a positive energized presence (PEP).

I am grateful that you have chosen to walk with me for a small part of your life's journey.

Take care.

Amit

Resiliencetrainer.com
Resilientoption.com

6

Contents

SMART:
An Introduction

1. The Problem

You can tell the state of humanity by what surprises you. Those norms keep changing. A few years ago, I saw a 70-year-old gentleman with advanced chronic lung disease. He had smoked since age thirteen. He shared that his mother would pack two cigarettes in his lunch box when he was in high school. "Take a few puffs during the break, son. It'll help you relax and focus," she would say. Cigarette smoking was a valued desirable practice in those times. Not so now.

Today, we aren't surprised to see greed, anger, envy, ego, hatred, and more—displayed live with full drama. What surprises us are acts of honesty, leaders displaying humility, politicians accepting a mistake, pharma CEOs decreasing the cost of medications. **Many of our brightest innovators are busy getting our kids hooked to a viral platform that can hijack our kids' brains and convert brilliant and focused students into zombies who cross the road with**

A few greedy among us are hurting countless millions

their heads buried in smartphones. We are creating a world where transient sensory pleasures are replacing the emotional joys of deep connections. We have become cognitively brilliant yet are emotional infants. These changes are killing us.

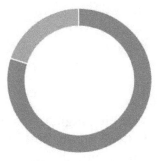

Most workers today experience excessive stress

I don't wish to paint a doom and gloom scenario. The reality, however, is that 80 percent of us feel stressed at work, 60 percent feel discriminated, 40 percent feel lonely, and 20 percent are depressed. Surveys show we are the most fearful we have ever been. We are also inventing new forms of rage—road rage, air rage, vending machine rage, low cell phone battery rage, computer crash rage.

We are losing our kids to suicide and drugs. A third of us struggle with chronic pain. Our life expectancy in 2018 was lower than in 2017. We are financially the wealthiest we have ever been, but emotionally and socially we are extraordinarily depleted. Our grumpiness is hurting the most important organ of our body—our brain.

We are shrinking two key brain areas—the pre-frontal cortex and the hippocampus, at the same time growing our stress-center, the amygdala. These changes affect important abilities like attention,

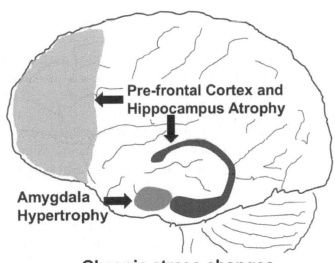

Pre-frontal Cortex and Hippocampus Atrophy

Amygdala Hypertrophy

Chronic stress changes the brain structure

judgment, decision making, memory, prioritizing, patience, keeping the

11

perspective, compassion, self-control, values integration, and more. The brain changes are making us irrational, unhappy, error-prone, unprofessional, impatient, disengaged, unhealthy, and addicted. In the process, we risk our lives and the wellbeing of everyone who depends on us.

These changes predispose us to a shift from complex higher-order deep thinking, to reflexive instinctive animalistic thinking and living. A significant concern is that after years of neuroplasticity, the brain changes become increasingly difficult to reverse, locking us into a state of high stress and burnout.

The problem of excessive stress, with all its downstream societal impact, is quite complex. The solution thus needs a multi-pronged well-thought-out comprehensive approach, bereft of individual biases and agendas. Sometimes, I like to use the example of the road, the car, and the driver.

The Road, the Car, and the Driver

Winter isn't my most favorite season for long drives. The sheets of black ice create a skating rink on the Minnesota roads. Let's talk about the three factors that affect our ability to drive safely and reach on time.

The road: A lot depends on the *road* conditions. Single-lane highways, a foot of snow on the road, sheets of black ice, no shoulder with a thousand-foot drop, large potholes—many different road conditions activate your amygdala. Further, I have no doubt that over the years, several impatient fellow drivers have shortened your telomeres. But you alone can't do much about the road conditions. While you can adopt a highway, you can't plow all the roads and certainly can't discipline every rogue driver.

The car: The second factor is your *car*. You can do a lot to keep your car in the best shape— keep the tires fully inflated, invest in winter tires, buy an all-wheel drive, keep your windshield defrosted, have working wipers, keep your brake pads and fluids in top shape. However, despite doing all this, if the third factor (the *driver*) isn't optimal, your drive would be unsafe.

	% Accidents directly caused	Your Influence over the factor
The Road Factor	2-5%	+/-
The Car Factor	2-5%	+++
The Driver Factor	90-96%	+++++

The driver: Research shows that human error causes a full 90 to 96 percent of the accidents. Perhaps you will agree that the *driver* factors are the most under your influence. **You want to make sure you aren't sleep or coffee deprived, aren't distracted, hurried, or hungry, and aren't driving with seething rage.** Anything that can hurt your focus and performance can cause unsafe driving.

The perspective on driving very closely applies to excessive stress. We can't, in short order, change the entire world and the people who live in it (the road). We can influence a bit, our organization, the people around us, and perhaps even our industry (the car). We, however, have a tremendous ability to help ourselves (the driver).

The driver factor becomes even more important when driving on a treacherous road with an ill-equipped car. Given that the stresses the world unloads on us these days will continue to increase in the coming years, upping our personal resilience is essential to thrive, and in some instances, even survive.

Based on the above, we can categorize most stress and resiliency solutions into two groups: Problem centric and Individual centric.

Problem-centric solutions **are targeted approaches that materially change the course of the ship.** At the organizational level, they include enhancing operational efficiencies, workload optimization, improving communication systems, eliminating waste, enlightening the leadership, cultivating a culture of thriving and excellence, and more. At the individual and team level, they include intelligent delegation, time management, simplifying the work, an optimal chain of commands, in-service training, among others.

***Individual-centric solutions* are focused and customizable solutions that help enhance individual resilience and wellbeing.** They include— lifestyle approaches (including diet, exercise, sleep, and self-care), mind-body approaches (including meditation, mindfulness, yoga), relationship-enhancing solutions (collegiality, professionalism, team building), meaning-centric solutions, resiliency training, and personal coaching.

A comprehensive approach to individual and organizational thriving integrates the following three components:
1. Understand the struggles, constraints, and strengths of the individuals, teams, and organizations
2. Innovate and implement problem-centric solutions
3. Innovate and implement individual-centric solutions

Understand the struggles, constraints, and strengths

Innovate and implement problem-centric solutions

Innovate and implement individual-centric solutions

None of these three components exist in a silo, and they support each other. An organization that has supply chain issues or a dwindling customer base is unlikely to recover from mindfulness training. Similarly, a burnt-out professional in the middle of a divorce who has a personal predisposition toward stress and anxiety is unlikely to bounce back with a five percent salary hike or sensitivity training. **We need both—thriving individuals and flourishing organization.**

The SMART approach primarily addresses individual thriving. SMART also provides insights into cultivating a more cohesive and productive team, through decreasing stress, and enhancing mindfulness and resilience. Further, through boosting individual and team resilience and wellbeing, SMART fosters organizational resilience.

2. Stress Management, Mindfulness, and Resilience

Time is an essential and useful construct that helps us organize life. Time, however, is also a source of tremendous angst. We often think of time when we feel a lack of it. We also feel time when the undesirable and hurtful dominate our experience. A healthy relationship with time is thus essential.

A complete solution that would help us better handle most life situations has to integrate all three time domains—the past, the present, and the future.

The Past, the Present, and the Future

A good driver integrates information from three sources—the rear-view mirror, the windshield, and what's happening inside the car. **The rear-view mirror shows the past, the windshield the future, and what's happening at the steering wheel is the present moment.**

The Past	The Present	The Future

The Three Domains of Time

Stress management is better handling what we see through the rear-view mirror. Resilience is being prepared for what is to come that we see through the windshield. Mindfulness is engaging with this moment on the road with a deeper presence and intentionality.

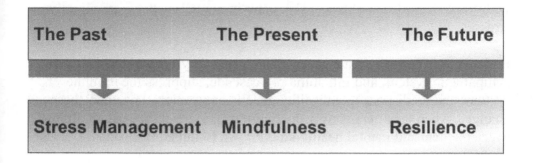

The Past	The Present	The Future
Stress Management	Mindfulness	Resilience

Stress management, mindfulness, and resilience are overlapping constructs that support each other. The separations I just shared are thus artificial. Nevertheless, the distinctions are useful to make sense of the terminology. Let's spend a few minutes with these three constructs before turning over to the SMART approach.

Stress 101

Stress is your struggle with what is, what was, or what might be. Stress is not liking what you have or not having what you like. Whenever the experienced or imagined is very different from the desired, we feel stressed.

Stress comes in three flavors—the good, the bad, and the ugly. *Good stress* **mostly relates to a change to which we haven't yet adapted.** A trip, a promotion, a new baby in the house—these are all good stresses. **Good stress is like salt in the food—it adds flavor to life. A meaningful purpose-drive life isn't possible without a healthy dose of good stress.**

Good stress turns into *bad* in three situations—a constant state of demand resource imbalance, a perception of lack of control, and when you can't find a positive meaning. A missed flight, constant work overload, a sick baby—are all examples of bad stress.

Stress turns *ugly* when it completely overwhelms us and robs us of hope. Getting mugged and assaulted on a trip, narcissistic supervisor at work

17

with toxic workplace politics, a sick baby in the ICU—these are all ugly stresses.

Bad and ugly stress activate hypothalamic-pituitary-adrenal axis, sympathetic system, and inflammatory cascade, suppress the immune system, and predispose to unhealthy genetic expression. Together, these changes, when they persist over the long-term, increase the risk of almost every medical and mental health issue known to humanity.

Stress has a particularly strong adverse effect on chronic medical conditions that drain 90 percent of health care dollars. Here is how it works:

- Stress adversely affects self-regulation, impulse control, and the ability to make good decisions
- Poor decision making leads to an unhealthy lifestyle (such as high-caloric intake, lack of exercise, tobacco use, excessive alcohol use)
- Unhealthy lifestyle causes chronic illness
- Chronic illness and unhealthy lifestyle, in turn, predispose to chronic stress

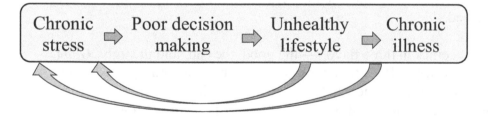

Finding creative stress-relief strategies is thus crucial to improving our physical, emotional, social, occupational, and financial health. Two approaches that can help mitigate personal stress are that of mindfulness and resilience.

Mindfulness 101

I like to define mindfulness as **living with intentionality, kindness, and gratitude**. Notice that the emphasis is on living rather than a discrete practice, on intentionality rather than present moment, and kindness and gratitude rather than non-judgmental stance.

I believe the currently understood version of mindfulness that emphasizes non-judgmental present-moment awareness, is difficult and also somewhat of a cliché. It is challenging to be non-judgmental because of the way the human brain is networked. **Better than non-judgmental stance is cultivating positive judgments of gratitude and compassion.**

Similarly, it is tough to anchor presence in the present moment. More useful and natural for us is to be intentional about what fills the present. **I believe mindfulness isn't about being in the moment. It is about *freedom* from the need to be in the moment.** I don't wish to be "in-the-moment" when getting dental work. If my wife wishes to plan our Friday, I can't say, "Honey I am in the moment right now. Can we talk about this later?" However, if you fill your moment with intentional gratitude and compassion, then it doesn't matter whether you are in the present, the past, or the future.

The present-day mindfulness calls for an integration of science, particularly neuroscience. It also calls for quitting the idea of emptying the mind. Instead, the modern mindfulness chooses to fill the mind with courage, hope, and inspiration.

I have spent considerable time rediscovering authentic mindfulness that can help us with our current challenges (mindfulness *v*2) and described it in a previous (rather lengthy) book, from which the table below is adapted.

Tenet	Mindfulness *v1*	Mindfulness *v2*
1. Insight	Focused on ancient philosophy	Focused on science
2. Presence	Anchored by time	Anchored by intentionality
3. Attention	Internally-focused meditation	Externally-focused meditation
4. Perspective	Zoomed in	Zoomed in and out at will
5. Attitude	Non-judgmental	Grateful and Compassionate
6. Practice	Mostly formal	Mostly informal
7. Anchor	Empty the mind; anchor it in breath	Fill the mind with courage, hope, and inspiration

In gist, I believe we need to reimagine mindfulness to align with the challenges we face in the modern world and not 2500 years ago. Such mindfulness naturally sprouts a most useful quality in our mind—resilience.

Resilience 101

Resilience is the core strength you use to lift the load of life. Resilience is doing well when you shouldn't be doing well. A more technical definition of resilience is: Resilience is your ability to withstand adversity, bounce back from adversity, and grow despite life's downturns.

The full flavor of resilience is better captured in stories, and not definitions. Think of someone you know who remains unfazed amidst a lot of rough and tumble. You admire that person's strength and values. Nobody can beat her or his spirit and love of life. That person is resilient.

Resilience prepares you to engage with what is, and what might be. Such strength calls you to be focused, balanced and anchored. Optimal physical health, a web of nurturing social connections, hope, courage, a belief in oneself, and a positive, uplifting view of the world and life—all help enhance resilience.

Several research groups including my team have consistently found that that higher resilience correlates with better physical and emotional health, better relationships, and greater success at work. Further, individual resilience contributes to team resilience, which in turn fosters organizational resilience. Given that the speed of the world will continue to accelerate in the coming years creating increasing cognitive and emotional load on our brains, I believe enhancing resilience is essential to decrease our stress and slow the tide of chronic illness and mental health issues.

Enhancing resilience, however, doesn't mean becoming a doormat, which has been an unfortunate conclusion of some researchers, particularly in healthcare. Instead, resilience is very forward-looking. Resilience gives you the strength to creatively solve your problems, raise your voice, and become the change agent. The opposite of resilience, burnout, takes away hope, confidence, and courage. **Burnout puts you in the downward spiral of life, while resilience lifts you into the upward spiral.** Elaborate and expensive organizational changes will go fruitless if the workforce is all burnt out. Hence the pressing need for resilience.

Choose the resilient option, to live an accomplished and purpose-filled life that spends most days pursuing an uplifting meaning, instead of running away from fear.

My goal in this chapter was to introduce you to the constructs of stress, mindfulness, and resilience. The descriptions above are by no means a comprehensive review. If you wish to spend more time with mindfulness and resilience, consider reading *Mindfulness Redesigned for the Twenty-First Century* and *Stronger: The Science and Art of Stress Resilience.*

Presently, the next rung in our journey is to co-discover a simple, scalable, effective and enjoyable approach toward decreasing stress and enhancing mindfulness and resilience, using the SMART approach.

3. The SMART Approach

The SMART approach integrates several disciplines, most prominently neuroscience, psychology, evolutionary biology, and philosophy. The approach also draws on wisdom from behavioral economics, anthropology, decision making, mindfulness traditions, positive psychology, and medicine. The insights from a number of these disciplines are synthesized into three core overlapping constructs—**awareness, attention and attitude.**

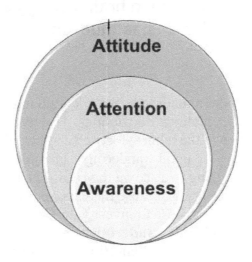

**The three core constructs
of the SMART program**

Awareness (Insight)

The core awareness is about understanding how our brain operates, notably how its instinctive operation depletes resilience and increases stress every single day. I like to call it the *theory of the brain*, which like the theory of the mind recognizes that **our thoughts, words, and actions are attributable to specific brain states.** Further, it also helps you understand that human brains are still evolving and struggle with multiple vulnerabilities. Specifically, three neural vulnerabilities collaborate to deplete our resilience. They are **focus, fatigue, and fear.**

**Most human brains struggle
with focus, fatigue, and fear**

Focus: SMART provides a modified network brain model as it relates to our attention, thinking, emotions, and actions. This model organizes our networks in two modes of the brain—focused and default. The *default mode* is the state of passive mind wandering such as driving home without registering anything you see on the road. The *focused mode* is that of directed attention either because the experience is intrinsically interesting or because you choose to invest your focus. Of late, **our brain spends a bulk of the day with wandering attention. Since wandering attention correlates with negative emotions, lack of productivity, and multiple medical and psychological conditions, decreasing the time in the default mode is likely to improve our health.**

Fatigue: Like most other body organs, after a period of activity, our brain needs rest. **Research shows our brain gets tired after 60-90 minutes of sustained effort.** Since brain fatigue speaks in subtle ways, such as a loss of focus, irritability, lower engagement, drop in creativity, and desire for coffee, when our brain gets tired, instead of resting, we push it further. Ultimately this can lead to severe fatigue, adversely affecting our performance, worsening physical and mental health, even causing early death. An excellent solution to prevent brain fatigue and mitigate its adverse consequences is to give your brain a few minutes of "creative rest" every couple of hours. I will share the specifics in the upcoming chapters.

Fear: One of the main tasks of our brain each day is to keep us alive and safe. **Our attention prioritizes noticing threats—to our physical, emotional, social, and financial wellbeing**. Our threat focus is compounded by our phenomenal connectivity that brings a daily dose of painful experiences in the world at our doorsteps (or inbox). Combine that with uncertainty, tremendous individual power to inflict harm on others, and our exceptional ability to imagine; we experience fears every single day. These predispositions force us to live in the 'prey mode,' even if there isn't an actual predator stalking on us.

This combination of distracted focus, brain fatigue, and instinctive attention to fear, generates and perpetuates stress. The first step in overcoming this predisposition is to become aware of why we struggle and recognize that we aren't alone in facing this. The validation that comes from learning about the brain's vulnerabilities provides people with the energy to move to the next step. The two-part actions in the next step are—attention and attitude.

Attention (Engagement)

When you go to a restaurant, you do not tell the server to get whatever. You look at the menu, gauge your appetite, preference, and cost, and then decide what to eat. You choose what you order and do not leave it to chance. Interestingly, **in our default state, we let chance determine what gets through our sensory system**. Given our predisposition to discount the good and inflate the bad, leaving our thoughts and perceptions to chance isn't a recipe for the healthiest, most productive experience. With this state of mind, we also risk missing out on spending quality time with loved ones or noticing the beautiful world that surrounds us.

Trained attention is a desirable alternative that gives you the option to choose what enters your conscious experience, at least for a few moments during the day. SMART recognizes that it will be near impossible (and undesirable) to control every sensory experience and thought. Instead, **SMART invites you to sprinkle moments of intentional attention, just for a few minutes during the day.** These minutes and moments are carefully chosen at certain times of the day to have an outsized impact on your attention, wellbeing, and relationships. We call them RUM moments (more on this later).

As the attention deepens and gets stronger, you can insert a creative pause in your experience that accords you the ability to invite more profound intentional thoughts, one guided by your core values.

Attitude (Mindset)

Our mindset is a set of beliefs we carry. Our beliefs, in turn, depend on our thoughts. Given that we can think about a situation in so many different ways, SMART offers a useful and uplifting construct to direct our thoughts—a bit like GPS for the mind. This construct has **five principles—gratitude, compassion, acceptance, meaning, and forgiveness**.

Despite their strength and value, none of these principles is individually sufficient. Together, they support and enhance each other. Gratitude alone can seem frivolous, compassion alone can deplete you, and forgiveness is extremely difficult without gratitude, compassion, and meaning.

Further, each of these principles is timeless, is research validated, and in combination can provide you with a perspective to overcome most life situations. You assign each principle a particular day of the week in the early part of training. As the training continues, each of these principles is accessible every day to help you rethink your challenges in a more adaptive productive way.

Research Evidence

Starting in 2008 we began testing the efficacy of the program in a variety of populations—physicians, nurses, students, support staff, attorneys, migrant workers, patients, and others. Chapter 33 on SMART research summarizes these studies.

SMART has shown positive results for several outcomes—resilience, stress, quality of life, mindfulness, anxiety, happiness, gratitude, life satisfaction, and burnout in about two dozen clinical trials. Practicing SMART has also resulted in an improvement in health behaviors and a trend toward a lower number of sick days. Some of the more recent studies are evaluating the effect on biological markers such as inflammatory chemicals, gut microbiome, and change in activity of the brain networks.

In the four sections that constitute the bulk of this book, I will elaborate on the summary presented above for the four modules: Gratitude; Mindful Presence; Kindness; and a Resilient Mindset. **Each module is a mix of two key ingredients—Insights and Practices**. Insights (awareness) are mostly about the vulnerabilities of our brain in the modern context, while the practices are designed to overcome these vulnerabilities. The practices integrate two key aspects—attention and attitude. The two parts of SMART support each other; insights help you prepare for the practices while practices help you develop deeper insights.

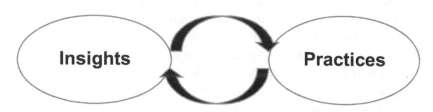

If you wish, you can obtain additional information about the program at resiliencetrainer.com and access the accompanying online program at resilience.mayoclinic.org. Let's start with part 1—Gratitude.

MODULE I
Gratitude

The first module strengthens and deepens your attention by focusing it on gratitude.

4. The Brain and the Heart

While every part of your body has a unique role and participates in the total human experience, the two body organs that run every aspect of your life and have the most significant effect on your resilience and wellbeing are your heart and the brain.

Your heart and brain together weigh approximately four pounds or just about 2.5% of the body weight in an average person. Those precious four pounds attract about 500 gallons of blood flow every single day, about twenty-five percent of the blood flow in our body (an equivalent of twenty-five hot showers). Our body has designed elaborate hard outer bony cases with soft inner lining materials to keep our brain and heart cushioned and safe so they can work undisturbed hosting and running our life.

Over the last 50-years, scientists have learned a lot about our four-chambered heart, the engine that powers each conscious moment. **The approximately two billion muscle cells in the heart work in unison to help it serve as an efficient pump, pushing 2000 gallons of blood through 60,000 miles of vascular channels each day.** Research has now established how the heart operates, how it is wired, and the logic behind its design. The heart is also relatively simple—its entire being is busy in one coordinated activity—receiving and ejecting blood. Our knowledge about the heart has revolutionized our ability to help it get strong and heal—with healthy lifestyle choices (proper diet and exercise) and optimal medical care. Surgeons can operate on the heart to help it beat stronger, even replace it if it ultimately fails at its job. I have seen hearts shocked into normal rhythm, valve blockages opened, fluid surrounding the heart removed, perforations repaired—all life-saving procedures that are truly miraculous. Cardiology and cardiac surgery sit at the pinnacle of modern medicine.

It's a different story with the brain. Ancient Egyptians didn't think much about the brain and discarded it in the embalming process. Aristotle believed that the brain was the radiator for the body—dissipating extra heat generated by the heart's activity. A lot has changed since then. We now know that our brain is a much more complicated design than the heart. *The brain is the most complex biological information processor ever built on earth, with approximately 86 billion nerve cells, 43 times greater than the heart.*

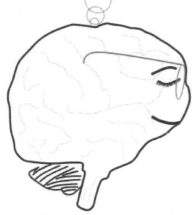

We are at an early stage in our understanding of the workings of the human brain

Nevertheless, with phenomenally improved computing power, over the past few decades, scientists all over the world have been collaborating to develop the operator's manual of the brain. It will take them several decades to fully figure it all out. But I don't have that kind of time, and I am sure you don't either. The good news is that we can vastly improve our brain's performance with what we know from the draft of the first few pages of that manual.

We'll shortly do two things. One, we will take a backstage tour of the brain to understand better what the brain is doing when you aren't watching. From that tour, we will learn how the brain operates and what brain mechanisms deplete our vitality every single day, both at home and at work. Just as you wouldn't drive your car not knowing how its steering wheel operates, you don't want to live your life not knowing how your brain operates. Second, using this knowledge, we will explore ways to get more mileage from our brain, so we are stronger, kinder, happier, more productive—in other words more resilient.

31

In the process, I will share with you the essence of all that I have learned in the previous 30 years in my journey pursuing greater happiness, mindfulness, resilience, and wellbeing. Let's start with the backstage tour of our brain next.

5. Brain 101: Focus

Your brain is a complex biological information processor, perhaps the most complex structure ever built by nature. The billions of parts (neurons) in this three-pound cantaloupe-sized mass are intricately interconnected to create a giant network with many subnetworks, like a big city. Any structure with so many connected parts is bound to have the potential for some glitches. These glitches adversely affect its operation and make it vulnerable, very much like the electronic gadgets we use.

We will not explore all the different ways that our brain malfunctions. Fascinating as that topic is, it is still in the early stages of exploration. Instead, we will study the imperfections in the brain's operation that emerge from these bugs. These imperfections collaborate to create the *three brain struggles—Focus, Fatigue, and Fear*. Let's explore them one by one.

Focus

When you are doing dishes, your brain isn't saying, "What a joy! I wish I could do this all-day long." Or, "Look at those silver-plated forks, they bring me such warm memories." Instead, your brain is busy thinking—about many things at the same time—children, work, home, finances, relationships, others. When thinking, the brain isn't saying, "My life is so blessed. I have the most wonderful kids, the best partner in the world, how come I have so much more money than I ever needed?" Instead, it is thinking about chores, hurts, regrets, concerns, fears—all the what ifs, could haves, should haves, often all at the same time.

It's the same story at work, particularly in a boring meeting. When I give a talk, I assume 50% of the people are checked out solving their life's problems in their head. I was once asking a dentist what proportion of the time his mind wanders when doing dental work. You'll be shocked—he said 80%. That is true for most professions.

And it isn't entirely people's fault. **Research shows an average person these days has over 150 unfinished tasks at any time.** When you see a dog poking his head out of the back seat of a car, he is experiencing the infinite fragrances of the world. What do you think the person driving the car is doing? Jumping from one open file in his head to the next—in other words, thinking.

In a series of research studies, scientists studied the activity of the human brain at rest. People were asked to lie down in an MRI scanner with their eyes closed and to think about nothing in particular. Until the early 1990s, scientists believed that like a calm baby sleeping in the bed, the brain would go silent when people are resting. When they peered inside the resting brain, their findings surprised the entire neuroscience community. Instead of becoming quieter, certain areas of the brain became very active at rest. It looked like a fish market. *Researchers realized when you are focusing on a chess game, your brain may be less active than when you are sitting doing nothing*.

On an MRI scan, blobs of blue and red (blue is blood flow decreasing, and red is blood flow increasing) appear and dissolve, like bubbles in hot water, or flickering Christmas lights. Those blue and red blobs are functional networks in the brain.

So, our brain is designed as a giant network of about 86 billion neurons. These networks organize themselves into two modes: Focused and Default. **All-day long, our brain sea-saws between these two modes.**

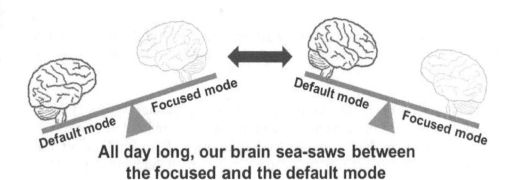

All day long, our brain sea-saws between the focused and the default mode

Let's start by talking about the focused mode.

The Focused Mode

Whoa! Ooh! Aha!—this is what the brain says when it is in the focused mode. What gets you to say these words? When something unusual and exciting happens, preferably pleasant. Like, watching Grand Canyon from 30,000 feet, having a creative insight, running into an old friend at farmer's market, or (if it ever happens) seeing a baby elephant playing soccer in your neighborhood—all of these activities and more get your brain in the focused mode.

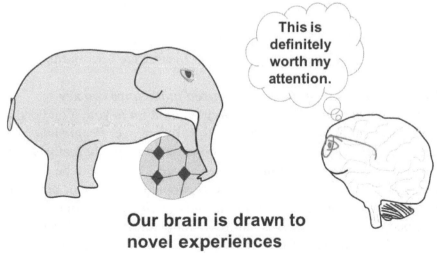

Our brain is drawn to novel experiences

Any immersive experience gets you in the focused mode. Playing with your kids, grandkids, nephews or nieces, reading a fascinating story,

35

bowling, or bungee jumping—they all get your brain in the focused mode. When bungee jumping, you don't say in the middle of the air—what was that email I had to answer?

Stepping on a broken glass bottle gets you to say another word—Ouch! Ouch, Yuck, Ugh, and Uh Oh, get you into a different kind of focused mode, one that you like to avoid. We will come to these in a little bit, but for now, think of an activity that you enjoy, during which hours feel like minutes, and you forget yourself for a sustained period. That activity puts your brain in the focused mode. When people talk about what they enjoy they often mention words like—reading, gardening, cooking, playing with kids, skiing, horseback riding, sowing, playing piano, and more. What do you find familiar in all these activities?

These activities pull your attention out of your head into the world, so you forget yourself. *We enjoy noticing, particularly deep noticing. We don't as much enjoy thinking*. I don't know of anyone sitting in the corner of a room saying—I am just going to think happy thoughts right now. The bulk of our thoughts tend to be neutral or negative.

You were a lot in the focused mode when you were a child—everything was magical. You could spend an hour making a paper plane or playing with a doll or toy car. You may have noticed at work that there are some projects and people you enjoy, while others you find bland. The key differentiator is how these projects and people engage your brain.

Projects that put your brain in the focused mode have two key features—they are interesting, and they mean a lot to you. You need at least one, preferably both the attributes to fully engage. *People who engage your brain's focused mode are ones who help you feel worthy, are resourceful, and tell you fascinating stories*. You like to be doing these things and spending time with these people because your brain loves to be in the focused mode. *The brain dreads getting bored*. In research studies, people gave themselves painful electric shocks in preference to sitting and doing nothing. Boredom and its expressions, Meh! or Blah! are equivalent of a different mode of the brain taking over—the default mode.

The Default Mode

Have you ever read a book, you read half a page and then say, what was I reading? If yes, where were you at that time? You were going through the motions—mind wandering. You had split attention, where what you were doing and what you were thinking was different. Guess how often we are like that during the day, with partial attention? Is it close to 10% or 80%? Most people say about 70-80%. Why is that?

Let's go back to when you were 16-year-old and learning to drive. What proportion of your attention capacity did you use in driving? Very high, like ninety percent. Would you have appreciated a phone call at that time? No, because you couldn't afford to get distracted. Your brain was busy making sure you didn't miss that stop sign and didn't annoy the instructor. But what about now? Now you can drive, sip music, listen to coffee, talk to someone, speed and look out for police car—all at the same time. Did you catch me saying sip music and listen to coffee? I was testing your focused mode!

So, what is the unused attention going to do if you are driving on a familiar road? Will you notice every blade of grass, branching pattern of the trees and logos of different shops? Or will you mind wander—thinking about everything at the same time? Unless I make an intentional effort, I do the latter and sometimes arrive home with no recollection of anything I saw on the road.

Driving is one activity that converts from focused mode to default as it becomes familiar. How about eating? Unless we knew there were flies in our soup or pizza toppings, we eat the first two bites and then have no idea how the rest of the slices disappeared. Food gets my attention when it is exotic, extraordinarily pleasant, or awful. I don't remember the last five minestrones, but I remember the guava ice cream I ate at an ethnic ice cream shop in Dallas. I also remember the one time we found a dead bug in our dish at a restaurant.

How about brushing teeth? Helping four-year-old brush her teeth can be fun if she complies. Even if not fun, it is engaging, since you diligently try to get each quadrant. Dental pain and cavities in a little child sound dreadful. But all that changes when we grow up. Did you spend the full two minutes this morning with your

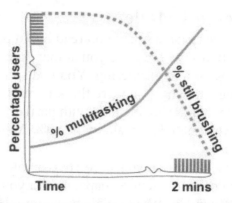

Most people do not brush for the full two minutes, while most multi-task while brushing their teeth!

toothbrush? Likely you gave up after 80-90 seconds. I have asked this question to over 50,000 people in the audience, in the U.S. and outside. Here are the results—*less than 5 percent of humans invest the full two minutes brushing their teeth in the morning*, irrespective of gender, race, nationality, or education!

Let me ask you another question about brushing teeth. Did you multitask while brushing your teeth this morning? If yes, you are amongst the majority!

The statistic for flossing is also humbling. *Nearly a third of us will prefer to do a mildly unpleasant chore, like ironing clothes or laundry, instead of flossing.* I believe only the activities that give us short-term pleasure continue to engage us for the long term. One idea is to couple a boring must-do activity with something enjoyable, such as listening to music or dancing. Why not sing, while loading the dishwasher?!

Another activity that converts from enjoyable to mundane is talking. What was the longest time you spent talking to your partner when you were dating? Must have been several hours. How about now? If you have been together for a decade or more, have you struggled to pay attention to your partner for more than a few minutes? Or else, have you struggled to engage your partner's attention for more than a few seconds? Does it ever happen that you tell three things to your partner and he or she looks completely blank?

I was once listening to a speaker when in the middle of the talk I panicked—I thought I had left the electric iron on at home. While the speaker was talking about heartburn, I was thinking about my burning home. I missed the entire presentation.

Anytime we are doing something that isn't novel, interesting, consequential, or entertaining, pretty much every repetitive protocol-driven activity, we get into default. How can you predict you'll be in default? A good thumb rule is when you are doing something you don't feel like doing, particularly if you have lots to think about.

Brain = Brawn

Here is what makes this worse. When it comes to changing/growing with use, our nerve cells aren't any more intelligent than our muscles. When you train a specific network of the brain with repeated use, the brain makes that network stronger (experts call this neuroplasticity—the ability of our brain to rewire itself with experience). **Unlike car tires that wear out with use, brain networks become stronger with use.** When you use a particular brain network, the brain says, "Oh! My owner just used this network. Let me serve him or her better by making it stronger." The brain's response isn't very different from a company that grows the division that brings it the most significant business.

Do you see a problem with this design? The more your mind wanders, the stronger your mind wandering apparatus; the stronger your mind wandering apparatus, the more your mind wanders. It's a positive feedback loop in which we get caught. The more we struggle to get out, the deeper we get stranded.

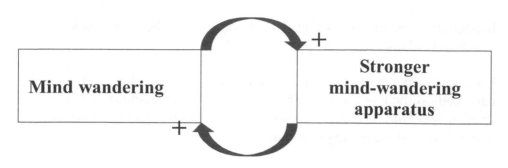

Most of the loops in our body are negative feedback loops. Thus, eating quenches your hunger. But what if eating increased your hunger? Won't you then be locked in a perpetual cycle of hunger-eating-hunger?

The brain's positive feedback loop helps us learn with experience but can also act like quicksand, trapping our attention. As a result, our mind wandering apparatus has taken over the rest of the brain. It is a bit like if you have a bowl of delicious soup and you add four tablespoons of salt in it. The salt takes over the taste of the soup.

Recognize that this isn't anyone's fault. It is an unintended consequence of our technological and financial success. We have built a complex, rich, interesting life at the cost of overloading our brain. The simple formula is:

Busy/Successful = Brain overload

An overloaded brain has lots to think about, which pushes our attention inward, getting us busy inside our head. We stop noticing the world around us. We also find it difficult to engage in meaningful connections with others. As I write these words and you read them, over three billion people are walking/driving around our planet barely aware of what's happening around them.

Anyone spending most of his or her day in the default mode cannot be happy, focused, creative, or think deep thoughts. *Families with members mostly in the default mode spend little celebratory time together* because even when in close physical proximity, they are mentally in parallel universes. Companies in which employees are in the default mode most of the day, will not do well long term. Such companies will struggle with absenteeism, presentism, high health care cost, difficult recruitment, and high turnover. *On an average, only 30 percent of the employees are presently fully engaged, partly because of the excessive default activity*. This impacts productivity, competitive edge, quality of the product, overall financial performance, and even viability of the company.

Excessive default activity also negatively affects your health. The higher the time you spend ruminating or mind wandering, the greater your risk of anxiety, depression, attention deficit, fatigue, and perhaps even dementia. Further, poor mental health is a proven cause of poor physical health.

It is the excessive mind wandering that makes you forget where you parked your car. I have done it many times. Forgetting where you parked your car is innocuous. Forgetting your toddler was in the car can seed a painful regret of a lifetime. In the U.S., we lose a baby once every ten days from forgetting the child in a vehicle. I can't think of a sadder example of excessive default activity.

Falling Behind

Gordon Moore, one of the co-founders of Intel described in a 1965 paper that the number of transistors in a dense integrated circuit would double every two years. In other words, computers will continue to get faster. Increasing computer speed coupled with their lower cost has increased the hustle and complexity of the world around us. The increasing speed and complexity are coupled with a biological constraint—*our brain is lodged in a hard skull and can't change that fast*.

Even though we have a very high capacity for long-term memory, we have a few bottlenecks in the brain. The two bottlenecks are our attention bandwidth (some experts believe we can only process about 100 bytes per second) and limited short-term memory. One person talking to you takes up about 60 bytes.

So, you are justified the last time you got annoyed when, right at the time you were talking to the utility company on the phone, your child kept on pushing his agenda to discuss critical details related to Halloween costume. Your attention bandwidth simply got overwhelmed. Similarly, we can remember only so many random items in the grocery list, and juggle only so many work-related projects at the same time. The other day I changed two passwords on the same day. It was a disaster!

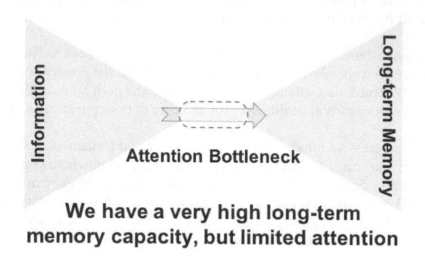

We have a very high long-term memory capacity, but limited attention

This separation between how fast the world is changing and how fast our brains can adapt leads to a constant state of cognitive and emotional overload. Study the accompanying figure carefully. You'll notice that the two lines (of change and adaptation) are diverging from each other at an accelerating pace. Perhaps you'll agree with me that we are collectively

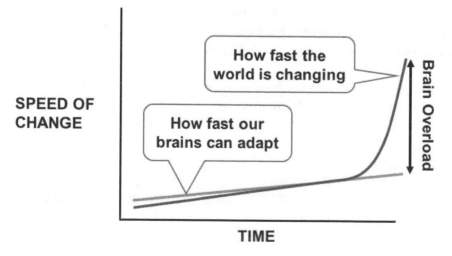

building technologies that have the unintended consequence of creating an overwhelming brain overload, that can undo the benefits of our technologies on our wellbeing, particularly our happiness.

Our excessive mind wandering isn't going away any time soon. The brightest brains on the planet aren't working on promoting forgiveness. At least not yet. They are creating the next generation of ideas that will get you hooked to their product. *Every distracting craving takes away our time from what is most meaningful—close relationships*. A deficiency of meaningful connections and constant mind wandering predisposes us to the second challenge of the human brain—fatigue.

6. Brain 101: Fatigue

Are there days when you feel completely wiped out by six in the evening? You want to be left alone to hibernate. If yes, what part of you gets tired? It isn't the liver, the gallbladder, or the spleen; it's the brain.

With respect to fatigue, we have two types of organs in our body—the first type are the energizer bunnies—they work 24x7 and do not get easily tired. The second type needs frequent rest. They sprint, get tired and need to rest so that they can run again.

An excellent example of the first type is kidneys. Kidneys work nonstop 24x7. You don't have to organize your day around the need to rest your kidneys. "Let's meet at 4:30. I'll be resting my kidneys from 2 to 4 PM." Further, our kidneys automatically respond to our needs. You don't have to tap your back and tell your kidneys—"Hey I just ate a salty pretzel. Will you please wake up and get rid of that extra salt?" Our brain belongs to the second type—it needs rest about every two hours and sometimes forgets to do its job.

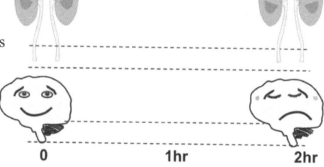

Research shows when you are doing something that needs intense focus, your brain starts fatiguing within 30 minutes and is exhausted by 90-120 minutes. If you

In a two-hour endurance race, our kidneys beat the brain

are doing something that is overwhelming, the brain could start getting tired within five minutes. Some researchers conceptualize a fatigue sensor in our brain that assesses the balance between effort and motivation/meaning. When the sensor perceives effort disproportionate to motivation or meaning, then it signals fatigue. For example, **aspects of the work that are repetitive and boring (such as difficult paperwork) fatigue you much quicker**, compared to planning fiftieth birthday celebration of your favorite relative.

Hurting in Silence

If you walk around lifting fifty pounds, within a few minutes, your shoulder and back will start complaining, "Stop I'm hurting." That's because they have pain receptors. You'll drop the weight to protect your body. Pain can be protective. But **your brain lifts equivalent of 200 pounds all-day long while giving only indirect feedback**. How does that feedback look like? Your focus deteriorates, you get irritable, you lose creativity, eat without hunger, and overdose on caffeine.

Why can't the brain give more direct feedback? The answer is simple and might surprise you. **The human brain that is hyperalert to pain in any body part doesn't have pain receptors for itself.** Neurosurgeons can operate on the brain while we are awake, without us feeling a thing. The result—**overloading our brain is much easier than overloading our shoulders**.

Our response to shoulder overload is to decrease the load. What do you do with brain overload—give yourself rest or push even more? Most people push even more. And this isn't an academic curiosity; it can inflict severe short and long-term damage.

Tired brains commit silly errors

Tired brains don't know how to be happy, creative, or productive. Initially, brain fatigue leads to a drop in performance—engagement and accuracy go down; reaction time and mistakes go up (the two figures that follow are adaptations from the findings of several research studies). You might say things you later regret and make decisions without thinking through them thoroughly.

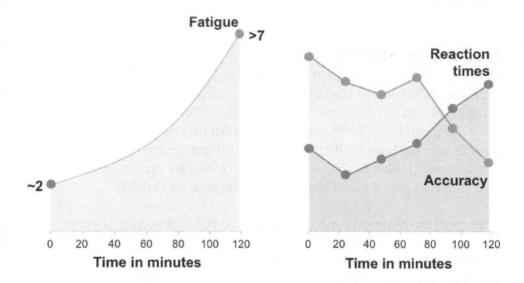

The brain fatigue leads to a drop in accuracy and an increase in reaction time

The brain fatigue increases the risk of mood disorders, accidents, worsens work performance, hurts relationships, and eventually predisposes to irreversible brain damage. Tired physicians miss their diagnosis, overworked surgeons don't operate well, fatigued drivers behave like they are drunk (without drinking), and exhausted spouses become snappy. Notice that all this is happening without you consciously noticing. Excessive work with related exhaustion also predisposes to premature death. Work-related death is called *Karoshi* in Japan and is considered a significant public health issue.

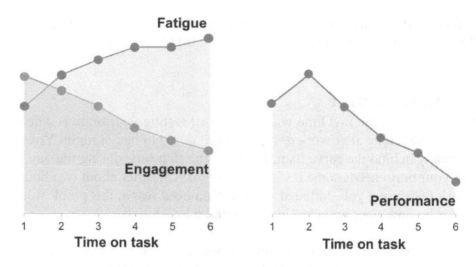

**Tired brains can't engage as well
resulting in performance decline**

Tired Eyes

The brain fatigue co-travels with eye fatigue . Our eyes also need rest after an hour or two of activity. **Six pairs of muscles move our eyes, and another muscle focuses our attention. These muscles need periodic rest**, which we often don't give if we are living a fast-paced day toggling between different screens. The majority of us on most days experience this demand-resource imbalance.

Our eyes weren't designed to look at a flashy screen three feet away hours on end. Our eyes work best when seeing different depths of perception and need periodic rest. They savor looking at color, nature, and sometimes nothing. Research shows **after an hour of looking at the screen, our tear film starts breaking, eyes start losing focus, and visual blurring occurs.**

A few businesses have built the biology of the brain and eye fatigue into their work schedule. For example, air traffic controllers stop working after two hours, and lifeguards after an hour or ninety minutes. But in most other professions our brains get pushed past fatigue limit. In an all-day retreat, if you are making a presentation after 2 PM, you are likely talking to people working with half their brains and 20/60 vision.

Behind the Curve

The chances are, the first time you think about resting your brain is when you get back home after work or right before going to bed at night. You are already behind the curve then. I believe the first time during the day when your brain needs some rest is at about 10 AM, after about two hours of work (assuming you started at 8 AM). You need rest at this point because by now your brain has accumulated a lot of gunk.

Your brain has trillions of nerve connections. Every time these nerves conduct, certain neurochemicals (like acetylcholine, GABA, and others) are released. These neurochemicals bind to the receptors, and this process mediates the nerve conduction. For efficient conduction, these chemicals have to be reabsorbed or metabolized, so the nerve connections are fresh.

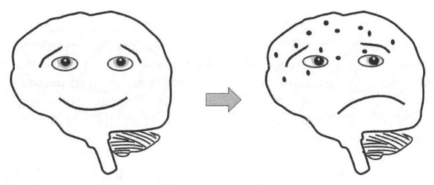

Beginning of the meeting   **After two-hours of meeting**

After a few hours of activity, the brain starts accumulating toxic chemicals that need clearance for optimal functioning. The eyes also get tired.

The clearing of nerve junctions is very much like the bowling alley where the pins have to be removed and placed again after each frame.

The problem is that all the neurochemicals aren't reabsorbed. After some time, your nerve connections look like your windshield does after a two-hundred-mile ride—littered with dead bugs. These unabsorbed neurochemicals interfere with the efficiency of transmission causing brain fatigue.

The solution to fatigue is to give your brain networks some rest so they can regenerate. From rest, I don't mean a 45-minute break. I imply a few minutes of "creative rest." Creative rest entails sprinkling your day with RUM moments.

RUM Moments

RUM stands for **R**est, **U**plifting emotions, and **M**otivation. A restful mind is content, free of conflicts, and not actively engaged in planning or problem-solving. No one would argue that we need to rest to rejuvenate our neural strength. Let's talk about uplifting emotions and motivation.

Our brain is the hungriest organ in our body. The brain feasts on two sources of nutrition—physical (oxygen and glucose) and psychological. Uplifting emotions and motivation are the brain's psychological nutrition.

Rest
Uplifting emotions
Motivation

Our heart and lungs do an excellent job of automatically providing the physical nutrients. But psychological nutrients aren't set for autofill. We have to choose to feed ourselves with uplifting emotions and motivation intentionally.

The reason rest alone doesn't work is because bringing the brain to a state of contentment and keeping it free of conflicts and constant planning is a challenging task. Such an effort will entail emptying the brain of thoughts which happens in deep sleep and meditation, but isn't easily attainable in the ordinary conscious state.

Easier than emptying the brain is to fill it with its psychological nutrition—uplifting emotions. An ideal uplifting emotion provides a sustained lift to you and is easily accessible. Gratitude for the people around you, for the good in your life, and for the bad that could have happened but didn't, is one of the lowest hanging fruits. Compassion that entails sending positive intentions to someone you care about or you know is struggling is another potent source. Reading stories about or meeting people who inspire you, finding reasons to be hopeful, sharing good humor, planning an exciting event, looking at old pictures or videos of friends and loved ones, doing a random act of kindness—these all can provide uplifting emotions. So can a stroll in nature, a good conversation where you felt heard, receiving authentic praise, and remembering you are loved.

Motivation, the M in RUM, is reminding yourself why you are doing what you are doing. Can you connect your work with a higher meaning such as people's lives changed, waste decreased, animals protected, customers entertained, students taught, people feeling safe, or something else that is uplifting? The more you can connect your work with helping an actual person, the easier you'll be able to find meaning in it.

Rest alone might take 20-30 minutes to recharge you. Rest mixed with uplifting emotions and motivation can restore you in less than five minutes. I have been personally sprinkling RUM moments in my day for the last almost a decade. (I will share the specific practices in a bit.) I can attest that my energy is 50% more than it was when I was ten years younger.

Another little trick I use, if my work entails a bunch of boring activities, is to **sandwich the boring work around two interesting or motivating activities**, even if they are only for a few minutes. Alternating boring with short interesting/motivating activities prevents monotony and may minimize error in the tedious task.

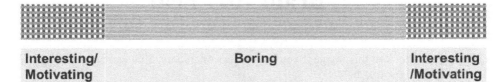

| Interesting/
Motivating | Boring | Interesting
/Motivating |

The boring task becomes easier if it is sandwiched between two interesting or motivating tasks

The focus and fatigue vulnerabilities of our brain are made worse by the third challenge—fear.

7. Brain 101: Fear

(Please do not look at this image if you have a fear of spiders. You can cover this image. I have repeated the text below)

Let's say you are sitting in your living room talking about Elk farms and wineries of the Midwest. Right then, you notice a big black spider climbing the wall. Will it draw your attention and prompt you to do something? If yes, it is because our attention amplifies any input that portends threat. Such attention saved our lives when we lived in the forests vulnerable to the elements, and still is needed, albeit less often in a suburban neighborhood.

(Repeated text: Let's say you are sitting in your living room talking about Elk farms and wineries of the Midwest. Right then, you notice a big black spider climbing the wall. Will it draw your attention and prompt you to do something? If yes, it is because our attention amplifies any input that portends threat. Such attention saved our lives when we lived in the forests vulnerable to the elements, and still is needed, albeit less often in a suburban neighborhood.)

What is likely to kill more people these days, spiders or donuts? Most people agree it is the donuts. When you go to a party where they have a box of donuts with 20 donuts staring at you, shouldn't you run away in fear shouting—"Run! They are trying to kill us by feeding donuts." Never go to Smith's party again because they tried to poison you with life-threatening cholesterol needles and sugar. Instead of becoming fearful though, we get attracted to donuts. We get attracted because our ancestors got drawn to calorie-dense food. We thus have some irrational attractions and irrational fears.

Irrational Fears

Fear has a bidirectional relationship with irrationality; **fear makes us irrational, and our irrationality (and related ignorance) breeds unnecessary fear.**

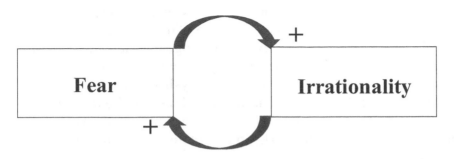

Fear makes us irrational, and irrationality breeds fear, locking us in a cycle of fear and irrationality

We do not fear what we should—such as texting while driving; while we fear what may be trivial—such as radiation exposure with flying. **Man-made risks (such as terrorism) evoke much greater fear compared to natural disasters (such as hurricane); sense of control decreases perceived fear (we feel safer while driving compared to sitting as a passenger); anything that puts our children at risk, even a small risk, is perceived more ominous than it actually is; new risks are perceived more menacing than existing risks (Zika versus Flu virus).**

Our **fear misperceptions lead to over-reaction to trivial threats and under-reaction to significant risks**—both can hurt us. For example, post 9/11, our fear of flying led to increased road travel. One research estimated that the increase in road travel caused a thousand more deaths than expected between October and December 2001. Fear of bioterrorism leads to indiscriminate use of prophylactic antibiotics, causing side effects and decreased effectiveness of the drug. On the other hand, not wearing seatbelts (20% of us still do not wear seatbelts) perhaps because we feel in control when behind the wheels, is a significant contributor to fatal road traffic accidents.

Painful Design

On top of all the external fears, our mind's exquisite vulnerability to emotional hurts causes enormous pain.

Let's say you step on a nail. What do you do—withdraw your foot or dig deeper into the nail? The obvious answer is to withdraw the foot. Now let's say you turn on the TV and they are showing news about a terrorist attack. What do you do, change the channel right away or get glued to it? Get glued to it, isn't it? Do you see how **our physical body is designed to withdraw from pain, while our mind is designed to dig deeper into the pain**? The impact of our mind's focus on the pain is made worse by the fact that **the same pain networks in the brain host emotional and physical hurts.**

**Physical and emotional hurts
activate the same pain network**

In its efforts to keep us safe, our neural architecture got crafted to maximize emotional pain. Our mind tells itself this story, "The more I know about the horrifying news, the safer I will be." And safety is paramount.

Our vulnerable design might not be a big deal if we lived in the modern-day equivalent of the Galapagos islands (for example, a monastery), totally safe from the predators, physical or emotional. But that isn't true for the majority of us. At every corner of the planet we have access to a limitless supply of negative news.

The resulting angst gets recycled and re-experienced several times by our phenomenal memory and imaginations. Think of a lion chasing a wildebeest. Either the lion succeeds, or the wildebeest escapes. If the wildebeest escapes, five minutes later, you'll find the animal calmly munching grass. Wildebeest's stress response starts fast and also exhausts quickly. The best we know, the wildebeest doesn't think about all the what ifs. Wildebeests also don't have 401ks, wills, or last wishes.

On the other hand, imagine a human being chased by a lion and escapes by the skin of his teeth. Will he be as relaxed five minutes later? Most likely he will be scarred for life. Our memory and imagination keep the experience fresh and recent.

A related challenge is that **for our brain, imagination is the reality. What we imagine, we experience as if it has indeed happened.** As a result, we relive the memory of the lion attack multiple times, with the same or worse adrenaline and steroid surge as the actual event, with the exception that the surge now isn't accomplishing anything. It is only making us more miserable.

And even if we try to forget about the pain half a world away, television and social media do a great job at keeping the echoes of bad events alive in our amygdala. The more you watch something on the TV, the more the channels repeat it, creating a perpetual cycle. Countless men and women suffer from unregulated fear invading into their present moment because of this painful design and the positive feedback loop.

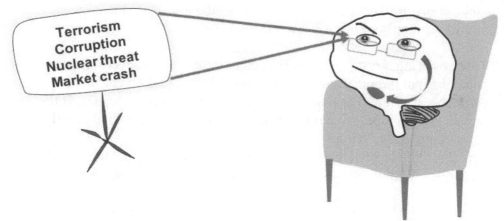

Toxic news has preferential access to our amygdala

A Speculative Theory

Let me share with you a speculative theory on why fear is so much in the air. Indeed, there are issues related to media presenting the most negative news, amplification impact of social media, and our connectedness—so we are bombarded with a lot of negative information. The challenge is we have also evolved to seek such information. Research shows **even those people who prefer not to watch negative news when presented with negative or positive press, notice the negative information more strongly.** Why is that?

Consider this—You had two ancestors. One was the happy-go-lucky type (Mr. H) and the other better-safe-than-sorry type (Mr. B). They were both standing in the forest and heard rustling sounds in the bushes 100 feet away. Mr. H thought it is probably a hedgehog, and I can keep munching on the berries. Mr. B thought it could be a tiger, let me take cover. A proportion of the time, it was the tiger. Mr. B found a safe spot while Mr. H didn't. Mr. B didn't have to beat the tiger; he only had to beat Mr. H. Enough number of such events, and the world gradually got populated with the better-safe-than-sorry beings!

Selective Recall

Allow me to test your memory of the threatening. Do you recall seeing a police car in the last week?

I haven't yet met anyone who didn't remember seeing a police car in the previous week. Most people remember additional details around that, like where the cop was standing, were the lights flashing, etc.

Next question—do you remember seeing a red Chevy in the last week? If not, then why not? Likely you crossed one of those cars. Here is the reason. Before you saw the cop, let's say your heart rate was 68 beats per minute. What happens immediately after seeing the police car, particularly if it is directly behind you? The heart rate goes up— 74…76…78, and then gradually settles. **Your brain remembers moments when your body has tachycardia (rapid heart rate) without exercise** through releasing extra adrenaline and steroids.

Our body doesn't like to experience tachycardia without exercise. Such tachycardia happens when we are made to feel vulnerable or unworthy. It is almost impossible to forget someone who insulted you. In a jiffy, I can create a list of people who made me feel small in the last twenty years. If I had to make a list of people who helped me, I would need much more time. Kids find it easier to make a list of who not to invite to their birthday party, compared to who to invite.

Moments of vulnerability and people who make us feel unworthy, even though they may be fewer than the positive ones, occupy a disproportionate real estate in our head. Of the 10,000 surgeries he has performed, my neurosurgery colleague remembers the four

As expected	Good	Bad (Loss)	
Just OK	Decent	Praise	Just OK
Good		Not too bad	Will work
Fine	Terrible (Insult)	Regret	
Praise	As expected	Nice	Fine	Like it

Negative memories occupy a disproportionate real estate in our head

that went bad. Such events are rehashed by our mind thousands of times, strengthening the brain networks that host them.

You have Many Hearts

We experience such micro-fears multiple times during the day. **You have as many hearts as the number of people you love.** If you are a parent of two children, you have two hearts beating outside of your body that you want to protect. But you can't be with them all the time, nor can you keep them in a bubble. The overwhelming feeling of vulnerability and lack of control that comes with this, along with the risks our kids take these days, keeps our adrenals pumping steroids, prevents deep sleep, and fosters mind wandering.

Many of your hearts beat outside of your physical body

Similarly, if you have a mean supervisor, every email from him or her will feel like a torpedo. If you have a troublesome neighbor, every sound coming from his direction will feel like an assault. It is the added load of these stressors that gets us. **We let the bad dilute the good; instead of empowering the good to dilute the bad.**

Most Fearful Ever

Surveys show we are the most fearful we have ever been. We fear corrupt government officials, think about the climate change, worried that bad things might happen to our loved ones, feel insecure about finances, and more.

We not only fear dark alleys, assaults, and terrorism, we fear pain, illness, rejection, loneliness, becoming inconsequential, and failure. **We are thus protecting our physical as well as the emotional body, more often the latter.**

When workers operate from a place of fear (and not seeking meaning), they push away success, and even if they succeed, do not enjoy their success. **Companies that operate from a place of fear, and not meaning, seldom achieve greatness.**

Fear hurts us in ways more than one, not just by causing stress and poor health, but also loss of compassion and broken relationships. When fearful, we pre-emptively attack others. On a global scale, **fear (and perceived unfairness) is often the starting point of wars** that have killed millions of people over the millennia. If you look at all the different ways fear affects our lives, I believe **fear hurts us more than the stuff we fear.**

None of this is meant to say that we shouldn't have appropriate fears. Living a carefree Pollyanna life is unrealistic and can make you vulnerable. **We can't shed our fears. We need to make our fears rational.** Be aware of your surroundings, take appropriate care, but once you are past the security check, then let your guards down, at least a little bit. If there is in-flight turbulence, trust the competence of the pilot, knowing that the probability that turbulence can bring down an aircraft is exceedingly low. That disposition will help you enjoy a free roller coaster rather than experience toxic adrenaline, the next time your airplane wobbles a bit through the clouds.

So, when you look at the source of our threats, we have many risks in the world, but compared to our forest dwelling ancestors, our society is much safer. Despite the barrage of negative news that jars us, the current crime rate is at a historic low, and our average life expectancy is near the highest it has ever been. **The bulk of our threats now are inside our head—hurts and regrets in the past and concerns and fears in the future.** I call them attention sumps.

8. Attention Sumps

I have shared the concept of attention sumps in the previous books (and in the online program) and will briefly recap it here.

Let's say you receive a call from your physician's office this afternoon. They leave a message on your voice mail, "Pam, call us ASAP. We need to tell you about a test result." You check the message in the evening. You call back, but nobody is picking up the phone. Will you be able to catch a sound sleep tonight? Unlikely, isn't it? Because you have an unresolved uncertainty in your head. As we go through life, we pick a lot of these uncertainties. The more you feel invested in the world and the larger the assets you are called to protect—both material and emotional, the higher your risk.

The strongest of these uncertainties, combined with regrets, hurts, concerns and fears, get deeply rooted in our psyche and become attention sumps.

The Four Layers

The four layers of attention sumps are formed in the following approximate sequence:

Step 1: Seeding the core: At the core is the original issue (regret, fear, loss, insult) most often related to past or future.

Step 2: Expanding the core: We think and overthink about our regrets, fears, losses, and insults, keeping them alive in our brain's circuits and giving them fodder to grow. We play out different scenarios of what might happen or what could have happened but didn't. I recently came across a young woman whose brother sadly took his life. He had struggled with depression all his youth and every evening she would talk to him to check on him and give a little boost of positivity. That particular day he called, but she couldn't take the call because she was in a party. He died that night of a self-inflicted gunshot wound. She will carry this regret all her life of how things could have been different had she picked up the phone.

Step 3: Thought suppression: In our process of overthinking, at some point we get exhausted and say, "I am not going to think about this anymore." That makes you think even more. **A suppressed thought recoils with a strong force.** When we try to avert a thought, we have to keep that thought alive in our mind, so we know what we are averting. In our effort to not think about something, we have to think about it, so we don't think about it. The result—we overthink and are caught in a closed loop. We, however, do not realize this paradox and keep chasing our tail all night long.

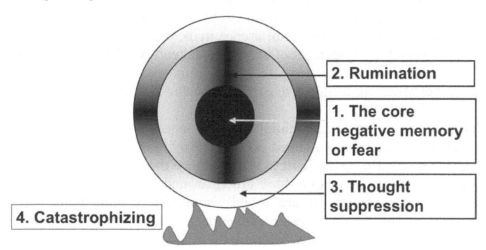

2. Rumination

1. The core negative memory or fear

3. Thought suppression

4. Catastrophizing

The four steps that create attention sumps

Step 4: Catastrophizing: Our tendency to globalize and catastrophize adds fuel to the fire. If you tell me you don't like my handwriting, I will assume you don't approve of me as a person. If my supervisor delays responding to my emails, I start wondering if I should start looking for another job. Like Mark Twain said, "I have suffered several terrible things in my life some of which actually happened."

Children, especially teenagers are particularly bad at catastrophizing. One bad grade and they feel their career is doomed. One negative comment on their social media post and they think they aren't popular anymore. This vulnerability can translate into anxiety and depression, social withdrawal, thoughts of self-harm, or even the ultimate step. I recently heard of a straight A student who excelled in every sphere but couldn't take the pressure, ended up taking his life. There were no warning signs whatsoever. Many of us bottle up negative emotions until they explode like a volcano. **Sometimes, it is good to let our kids vent. Perhaps they need that outlet, so they don't bottle up their emotions. Venting, I believe is better than suppression.**

Grumpier than Others

Recognize that some of us are genetically predisposed to feel grumpier than others. Our brain's design is laid out by a combination of genes, the variations in which can make a difference in the reactivity of your amygdala and the engagement of the prefrontal cortex. These differences also affect the neurochemicals bathing our brain. All of these genetic influences affect our tendency to generate the attention sumps.

Combined with that are early childhood experiences. **The brain in early childhood is like freshly poured concrete. Any mark on it can leave a long-term scar that is difficult to remove once the concrete dries up (the adult brain).** Many of us have grown around selfish, abusive people who didn't know how to nurture a child's brain. The resulting scars predispose us to convert short-term adversity into attention sumps that interrupt the flow of life for a long time.

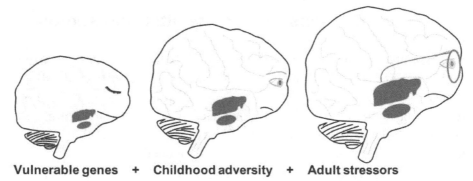

Vulnerable genes + Childhood adversity + Adult stressors

The three strikes that activate the brain's centers for negative emotions and cause mental health issues

Awareness of genetic and early childhood influences on the brain's design and functioning has helped me nurture kindness toward others and self. **Uncoerced kindness that spontaneously emerges from the realization of others' vulnerabilities offers a wonderfully calming perspective.** With kindness, we come to a place of acceptance, acknowledging that as we live our life, most of us will develop attention sumps—few or many, small or large—depending on our vulnerabilities. Such acceptance will weaken the hold of these sumps, so they haunt us less at 2 AM in the morning.

Trapped in Attention Sumps

When I ask the audience, how many of you have cried in the previous six months because of physical pain, a few raise their hands. The same question about emotional hurts raises many more hands. **We spend more time protecting our emotional body than our physical body.** And infinite are the ways we can get emotionally hurt, from the happenings of the past and the present, and the imaginings of the future.

The default state of wandering mind makes all of this worse because wandering mind is a symptom of weak attention, and **weak attention gets easily pulled by the suction of attention sumps.**

Further, powered by neuroplasticity (the brain's ability to change with experience), every time we visit attention sumps, we add more material in them, thereby making them stronger. Neuroplasticity provides the fodder to the whirlpool that traps many of us. As we live life, our mind gets filled with a lot of these sumps, they color the present moment, and make our life dull.

The attention sumps suck tremendous energy and vitality every single day. It is tough to be happy when you have a lot of these. **Too many attention sumps in the past predispose to depression, many in the future predispose to anxiety, and the ones in the present cause unhappiness.**

The sad part is that people often don't realize how much they are struggling until they come out of their struggles. Even when they

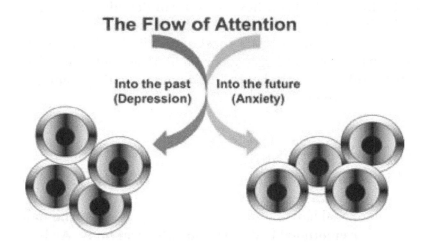

The Flow of Attention

Into the past
(Depression)

Into the future
(Anxiety)

Attention sumps in the past predispose to depression, in the future predispose to anxiety

understand, the majority don't have access to help.

There is no escaping attention sumps. Annihilating them isn't our goal either. **Our goal is to create fewer of these in the future, stop adding fuel in them today by visiting them less often, and whenever feasible, look at them differently—as opportunities for growth.** We also strive to avoid negatively judging people whose life situations trapped them into too many sumps. Compassion is much healthier and rational—for them as well as for you.

Let's summarize the central insight now. Then we will move forward with the first set of skills.

9. The Main Insight

The default state of both our brain and heart isn't satisfying. When you don't train your heart, the resting heart rate increases and your heart muscles fatigue quickly. When you don't train your brain, resting thought rate (i.e., mind wandering) increases and the brain fatigues with just little effort. Our brain's primary task, which is to keep us safe, makes this worse. Our untrained brain's obsession with fear sacrifices peace and happiness. All this occurs backstage but colors the drama happening front stage.

We need not be afraid of fear. I think our greatest peril is in our irrationality and ignorance that drives our fears. We deploy our energy where we don't need to (like getting angry with the weather or slow internet) and do not use our energy where we should (like physical exercise or building relationships). Our irrationality is equivalent of calling 911 for a neighbor lighting up a sparkler, but not worrying about a large fire in our living room. **Our brain was perfect for survival in the world that was fifty thousand years ago. But our brain's automatic operation is quite maladaptive in the twenty-first century. Our every negative feeling hurts our entire body, particularly our heart and our brain. Similarly, our every uplifting thoughts and feelings help our being.** Hence the need to take charge.

We need to take charge of our brain and allow it to learn from the collective wisdom that has emerged from the collaboration of millions of brains of scientists and sages on our planet. We have taken charge of the evolution of our physical world. Unlike any other animal, we are combining different forms of matter, creating entirely new arrangements that nature would never have been able to produce in a billion years. **In this world where intentionality has taken over natural evolution, we have to use the same intentionality to craft an emotional revolution.** That is the path to resilience. Short of that, we will live in a beautiful world with a miserable brain.

I eat healthy, exercise, and sleep well. How else can I help my heart doctor?

Feel hopeful, cultivate patience, nurture deeper relationships, better manage your fear, and live with purpose. Every one of your uplifting thought and feeling helps your heart.

Every one of your uplifting thought and feeling helps your heart

Just as when you take charge of your heart, you build strong heart muscles (resilient heart), when you take charge of your brain, you build strong brain networks (resilient brain). A resilient brain has two key attributes:

#1. Strong, focused, deep and intentional attention

#2. A mindset that is

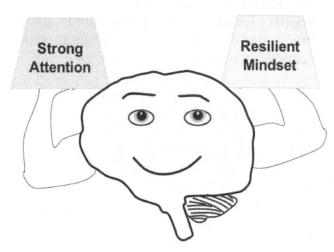

Strong attention and resilient mindset carve a resilient brain

driven by your core values i.e., a resilient mindset

In essence, training your brain is engaging its focused mode and persisting in your efforts until the brain's focused state becomes its default. Such a brain spends the bulk of the day in a state that can be best captured in three words—positive energized presence (PEP).

Positive Energized Presence (PEP)

PEP isn't a Pollyanna state of unbridled positivity. Instead, PEP is authentic engagement with what is. PEP recognizes the negativity but doesn't let it overwhelm the day. PEP finds the right within the wrong, is compassionate toward others and self, and instead of running away from fear, chases a meaning that serves the collective. PEP fosters courage, rational hope, and inspiration.

You immediately notice people whose brain embodies PEP. Even a short meeting with them leaves you uplifted and inspired. You look forward to spending time with them; are excited to see their name on your calendar. They enhance your self-worth. SMART aspires to help you nurture such an inspiring presence on most days.

Creating a brain that effortlessly embodies PEP, however, can only happen in small steps since the old brain won't give you back control that easily. That's why **SMART starts with brain micro-workouts that are only one to three minutes long.** Each such micro-workout offers you a combination of relaxation, uplifting emotions, and motivation (remember RUM), providing you with both calmness and energy, and engages deeper attention. An optimal combination of relaxation and activity energizes your brain.

We have kept several considerations in mind in designing the RUM moments:
- Time efficiency
- Align with 21st-century living
- Pleasing in the short term
- Keeping it novel (avoid clichés)
- Keeping it simple

- Broader life impact

Integrating these aspects in the design, we have identified some specific practices and moments of the day when even a small investment of time and effort can offer a remarkable benefit.

The first such moment is right when you wake up in the morning. If you change how you wake up, you can change your entire morning. Thus, the first core practice that will take two to three minutes of your time is at the most vulnerable and opportunity-filled moment of the day—right when you open your eyes and are ready to meet the day.

10. Morning Gratitude (Core Practice #1)

It's about 5:45 AM and I have just woken up. A long day lies ahead, but it can wait. The first two minutes of the day are mine. I close my eyes pretending to be asleep and think about my wife, Richa. She is sleeping by my side. As her loving face flashes in front of my eyes, I attempt to recall one good thing she has done in the previous 24 hours. I think about her patience with our 14-year-old last night. A smile comes to my face as I send her silent gratitude for being in my life.

Next, I think of my father and try to recall my first memory of him. I see him walking into the house with a bag full of groceries, mangoes, oranges, and dates bulging through the plastic. I send him silent gratitude.

I then think about my niece, Nina. I recall the color of her eyes—dark brown—and send her silent gratitude.

I think about my colleague Brent who has been such a support for my work over the years. I send silent gratitude to Brent.

I think of my friend Dave who has passed away. I recall the last moments I was with him. I give him a virtual hug and then send him silent gratitude.

And then I open my eyes, ready for the day.

> **Core practice #1: First thing in the morning, think about five people in your life who mean a lot to you, and send them your silent gratitude.**

I like to wake up each day thinking thoughts of gratitude. The first person I think about is usually my wife even though she may be sleeping by my side. The first person she thinks about (I hope!) is me! This practice has transformed our mornings. I wake up with better focus, feeling relaxed, connected, and experiencing uplifting emotions. It gives me a context to the day, fills me with energy, and improves my relationships. Biologically, I look at this as waking up with oxytocin and endorphins.

Before I implemented this practice, I used to wake up with adrenaline and steroids. Within a few seconds of waking up, I would start mind wandering or check my phone. My heart would race thinking about what lay ahead. Almost invariably an attention sump would creep into my head, waking me in the "prey mode" feeling vulnerable.

I have personally not met more than five people in my life's journey, who wake up intentionally in the oxytocin/endorphin mode. Your mind's state in the early morning hours is important to your wellbeing; the surge in adrenaline and steroids first thing in the morning is partly the reason for our highest risk of heart attack, stroke, and sudden death early in the morning. One of my life's mission is to help people wake up grateful, not grumpy.

Do you have someone in your life who is priceless to you? I am sure you are worth trillions to someone. I urge you to **think about your trillion-dollar net worth first thing in the morning and not other more trivial matters. Do not leave the bed until you have remembered five people in your life you are grateful for and sent them your silent gratitude.**

A Good Question

You might ask, why just people? Why not focus on breath, be grateful for health or success, or a warm home? That's a good question and certainly those aspects will be fine. In developing this exercise, I started with a focus on the breath. It worked for a few weeks and then got boring. I then tried focusing on relaxing my physical body, then started noticing the room, dwelled on success and health, but found that each of these practices become dull very quickly. But practicing with people never faded. I can look at my mother's eyes for a million times or visit the OB room holding our girls, right after they were born, countless times and not get bored.

Sometimes I consider the morning gratitude practice a combination of candy and Aleve. It gives me immediate positive feelings like candy and the effect lasts for several hours like Aleve. I also value the added benefit of improved relationships. A lot may be going on in mine and my wife's lives, but as long as we feed each other with positive energy and work as a team, we will be OK. I have noticed the quality of my relationships have improved with people who I have thought of in my morning gratitude.

Does it have to be right after you wake up? Preferably, but not necessarily. The chances are if you do not practice it right away, you will forget. That's why I suggest placing a post-it note on the bathroom mirror with the word gratitude written on it. **If you forget this and find yourself in the bathroom, when you see that note, then go back to bed and start over.** Other ways to remember is to put a collage of people you are grateful for in your bedroom, or a gratitude sticker on your smartphone.

If you forgot morning gratitude, then go back to bed and start over!

The intention, however, is not to be rigid. If you already have a contemplative/spiritual practice such as prayer first thing in the morning, then you can do the gratitude practice in the shower, if you prefer. Also, the morning gratitude practice

Put a gratitude reminder on your bathroom mirror

isn't just for the mornings. You can repeat the practice later in the day. No matter how busy your day, practice sending silent gratitude to a few people in your life before you fold the day.

A Few Additional Ideas

Here are a few additional ideas to help deepen and sustain the practice:

- If you worry about the people you are sending silent gratitude to, then **assume that by sending them gratitude you have protected them for the week.** It will help you feel better and also create subliminal guilt if you forget to do the practice the next day, which will keep you going!

- If you have a family of eight, you don't have to stop at five and feel bad rest of the day.
- On a busy morning when you have only 11 seconds to spare, think of only one person before you get out of the bed.
- **Pets are welcome; they are family.**
- As your practice deepens, you can also invite someone you want to have a good relationship with, but are currently struggling. The practice might help improve your relationship with that person.
- Consider including someone from work on your list. It will help you cultivate a more rewarding relationship with your colleagues.
- If you have to pick from among a large number of people, then plan, make a list the night prior, so the practice is easier next morning.
- If you can't think of five people, be creative. Perhaps you can be grateful for all the ladies who came for your mother's baby shower before you were born. You can think about your physician or nurse, and the teachers who taught them. If this seems far stretched, then limit to the smaller number with whom you feel comfortable.
- **The only known side effect of the practice is that you might fall asleep.** So, keep a backup alarm if that is your concern.
- You can choose to practice slow deep breathing during the practice to obtain a greater relaxing effect.
- Add a small stickie on your smartphone with the word gratitude written on it to serve as a reminder.
- Partner with someone and hold yourself accountable to each other.
- Create a small reward for sticking to the practice for the week.

This simple two minutes of commitment to remembering people in my life has transformed my mornings, as it has for many others. It has deepened my attention, trained my brain's focused mode, gifted me positive emotions, and improved my relationships. I miss it the day I forget to do this practice.

Try it initially in the way I have shared it. As you become familiar, tweak it in ways that work the best for you, so you make it yours. Consider what I have shared as a recipe. Add or remove a few spices depending on your personal preference. You are more likely to stay with this practice if you make a few changes to customize it for you and commit to someone who cares about you, that you'll do the practice, at least for a week. Why not make a commitment right here by texting yourself the note below?

> **Starting today, I commit to practicing morning gratitude every day of the week for the next one week.**

A subtle but important point to remember is that this practice is geared to train your attention, so your attention is deeper and more intentional. We aren't just bringing greater gratitude in life. **We are strengthening our attention by focusing it on gratitude. Developing strong attention is the first and most important step toward sculpting a resilient brain.**

Gratitude at Work

Work is a lot about relationships. **The single most potent resilience drain at work is difficult relationships (and toxic workplace politics).** Adding gratitude to the mix won't undo your supervisor's attitude but can help elevate your burnout threshold. Here are three ideas I practice for bringing greater gratitude at work.

#1. Include work colleagues in the morning gratitude practice—**You start seeing more positive qualities among people who feature in your morning gratitude practice.** Including colleagues in morning gratitude is an effortless but highly beneficial way of enhancing collegiality at work.

#2. Focus on gratitude before a meeting—**One of the best ways to prepare for a meeting is to remind yourself why you are grateful to the person you are going to meet.** A grateful disposition is particularly helpful for an adversarial meeting. When you carry the energy of gratitude, your facial expression, the overall demeanor, the energy you share—all changes. These changes are infectious and touch others in the room, bringing adrenaline down a few notches.

**Gratitude helps you carve a
more thoughtful response**

#3. Feel grateful for the privilege of having a job—Sometimes we get too fixated on the minutiae. If I am not running this project or that project, my work isn't worthwhile. Such an approach runs the risk of limiting your possibilities. Instead of the minor specifics, if we can be grateful for the privilege of having a job and consider everything else a bonus, then I have no doubt we will find greater meaning in the work we do. Such meaning will enhance engagement, and in the long run, bring us the projects we find most worthwhile.

The gratitude practices I have shared above are in the privacy of your mind. Gratitude shared can become even more powerful. Let's talk about that next.

11. Gratitude Jar

I cannot overstate the value of humor in life. Humor and its cousin laughter lowers blood pressure, improves heart health, and enhances immunity. Laughter is extremely helpful in improving mental health and enhancing social connections. **The hearts that laugh together beat together.** The benefits of humor might multiply if you connect it with gratitude, particularly in the context of family and work environment. The next practice, gratitude jar, combines humor with gratitude and relationships. Here is how I have done it.

On a side table in our home is a simple jar with some scratch papers and a pen. Before going to bed, I often stop and think about one good thing that happened during the day or one bad thing that could have happened but didn't. I try my best to add humor to that situation, write a brief note on a scratch paper and toss it in the jar. A few examples of stuff I have been grateful for are: "I didn't floss this morning but haven't lost my teeth yet." "Got away with making a bad ponytail for our five-year-old." "Glad the sandwich tasted so bad, I didn't exceed my calorie goal for today." Try not to force humor, let it flow naturally. After a few weeks of doing this, read a few of your previous writings. Not everyone can find the time to write each day, but all are welcome.

After a few weeks of collection, these notes can be great conversation starters at the dining table. At the end of the year, you can paste a selection of these writings and create a collage.

Perhaps you can take a picture of the collage and send it out as a new year card to your closest family members to show them your life's lighter side. You are creating a small legacy.

Here is one from me:

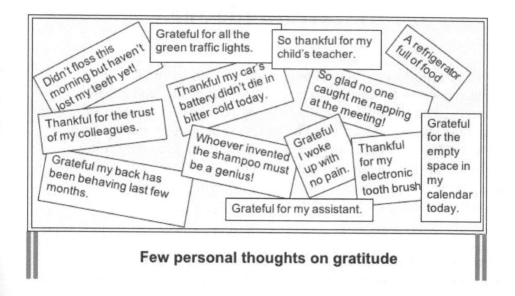

Few personal thoughts on gratitude

What you search for, you find. What you find, comes to dominate your conscious experience. If you choose to think about what went right, you'll discover more of it. I believe it is necessary to cultivate that instinct in a world where billions of dollars are invested every day in bringing you information about what went wrong. We can't blame just the media companies for this. We learned earlier that research shows even people who prefer to hear the good news pay greater attention to the bad news. Greater attention on the bad news is particularly true for those who like to remain abreast with the latest events. **The bad news is often perceived as more actionable compared to good news and thus of greater importance to attend.** You'll have to intentionally break this negativity cycle, at least for a few moments during the day.

The more you can involve children in this practice, the better. The gratitude jar will be a fun way to introduce them to gratitude. Adding light humor is essential to invite their participation. Try not to direct your humor at any particular person. Instead, learn to laugh at life, and of course at yourself. **I believe if I don't laugh at myself, someone else will!**

12. Summary

As a reminder, the core practice in module I is:

> **Core practice #1: First thing in the morning, think about five people in your life who mean a lot to you and send them your silent gratitude.**

Practice this at least for a week, before adding a second practice from module II. Here are the four key learning points I wish to recap before moving to module II:

1. The seesawing brain
2. Take charge
3. Wet your feet with gratitude
4. 1+1=11

The Seesawing Brain

Our brain seesaws between two functional modes—Focused and Default. The focused mode is intentional while the default is automatic. Intentional needs effort; automatic is effortless. That's the reason default dominates most of our day.

Our brain's default operation keeps it unfocused, fatigued, and fearful. In this setting our attention is superficial, we experience excessive stress, and lack hope and inspiration. Our adrenaline and steroid levels are high, oxytocin and endorphins are low. The result is a rise in the inflammatory markers, immune suppression, metabolism favoring diabetes, and impaired anticancer surveillance. We risk falling sick. Indeed, research shows almost every single aspect of your health—risk for new illness, disease prevalence, the degree of symptoms, response to treatment, complications, and overall longevity—all are negatively affected by excessive stress. Excessive stress also predisposes to addictions, disrupts relationships, impairs creativity, focus, and productivity, increases errors, lowers professionalism, and increases turnover at work. **Our brain's default setting makes us sick and leaks resilience every single day.**

Take Charge

Our body has two different types of organs—the first type is best left alone to do what they are doing; the second type needs lifelong training and maintenance to be in optimal shape. Liver, kidneys, gall bladder, intestines, and spleen belong to the first type. You won't find too many gall bladder wellbeing centers or the center for spleen health.

The second type are the heart, muscles, skin, and the brain. They need lifelong care to stay in shape. We all do a little (or a lot) for our skin, particularly our face. Just as your skin needs moisturizing to look good and healthy, and your heart and muscles need a workout to remain strong, your brain needs regular care to stay resilient.

The brain needs workout of its networks that host intentional attention, think profound intentional thoughts, and create uplifting emotions. You will have to literally "take charge" of your brain, so you overcome its lifelong habit of superficial attention, mind wandering, and negativity bias. Taking charge will entail thinking thoughts and speaking words that seek a higher meaning.

The problem is the brain won't cede control that easily. If you don't believe me do this little practice. Look at a clock and follow the movements of the second's arm for 60 seconds without letting your mind wander. Alternatively, again without allowing your attention to wander, slowly read all the ingredients from the label of one of your shampoo. Make sure your attention remains focused on the label, and you understand each ingredient. Here is a list from one of the popular brands:

Pyrithione Zinc 1%. Inactive Ingredients: Water, Sodium Lauryl Sulfate, Sodium Laureth Sulfate, Glycol Distearate, Zinc Carbonate, Sodium Chloride, Sodium Xylenesulfonate, Cocamidopropyl Betaine, Fragrance, Dimethicone, Sodium Benzoate, Guar Hydroxypropyltrimonium Chloride,

*Magnesium Carbonate Hydroxide, Methylchloroisothiazolinone,
Methylisothiazolinone, Blue 1, Red 33.*

The first time I tried this, my attention wandered a few times. It made my
head hurt. What I learned was that I couldn't force my attention to focus
for more than a minute or two, unless what I was attending was very
interesting and enjoyable. Extrapolating that learning to SMART, more
practical than a 45-minute practice is two to three-minute practice.
Further, **more engaging than breath, word or still image is attention to
people who we know care about us.** Hence the idea of taking charge of
your brain and training your attention by focusing it on gratitude, two to
three minutes at a time.

Wet Your Feet with Gratitude

Gratitude is like water—most precious and yet widely available.
Embracing gratitude is one of the simplest and most powerful approaches
to enhancing your wellbeing. That's why we start with this universal
emotion. Instead of waking up with wandering attention, wake up
thinking of your trillion-dollar net worth. Replete yourself first thing in
the morning. Share it with the family or work colleagues by keeping a
gratitude jar. Express gratitude to people who have helped you become
who you are today. Gratitude will fill your mind with positive emotions.
It will clear your focus, help you be happier, enhance relationships, and
improve physical health. In one study gratitude even increased personal
income. Gratitude comes with no known side effects like skin rash, GI
upset, or sleep disturbance.

One of the best ways to bring more gratitude in your life is to lower the
threshold at which you feel grateful. In this context, I recall seeing a
patient with kidney failure several years ago. I was a medical intern at
that time. He called me and shared two things that would have made him
happier that day. One, if his kidneys were to wake up and make a bladder
full of urine, and two, if he was able to walk to the bathroom to void it. I
realized that day that **best not to wait for something big to happen to
feel grateful. Instead, find gratitude in the mundane and easy—the
ability to walk, taste, touch, feel, think, smile.** Such gratitude will help
me be grateful for even adversity, that will make me very resilient.

I know of no path to authentic happiness that doesn't have the gratitude milestone. Create a discipline, make this into a habit, and partner with others to pull them into gratitude.

1+1=11

A wise old saying I grew up with was that **1+1 ≠ 2; 1+1 = 11.** One of the best ways to deepen your practice is to partner with someone—your spouse, friend, colleague, neighbor, grownup child— anyone you think will help you remain disciplined and will be

willing to grow with you. Pick someone whose values are closely aligned with your values. If you partner with someone who is allergic to gratitude or compassion, then you will struggle to find common grounds.

Gratitude and Resilience

How can gratitude enhance your resilience? Your resilience has two sources—inner and outer. Attention to gratitude helps with both. From the inside, **gratitude fills you with positive emotions, giving you extra energy that can help you better handle adversity. Gratitude helps plug the energy drain from a problematic situation.** From the outside, gratitude for people improves your connection with others. The more you feel connected with others, the more supported you feel. All of this gives you a better sense of control, find greater meaning in life and **look at obstacles as worthy challenges rather than threats.** These are core resilience attributes.

In general, I suggest practicing morning gratitude for at least a week before moving to part 2, Mindful Presence. In part 2 I will share with you what brought me into studying resilience. We will then learn how getting your loved ones suspicious of you can be a good thing!

MODULE II

Mindful Presence

The second module, mindful presence, strengthens and focuses your attention by guiding you to notice the novelty of the outside world that hugs you at each moment.

13. My Story

June 1995 was when I came to the U.S. As I was landing early morning at the JFK airport in NY, I thought everyone must be happy and resilient here. I had good reasons to believe that. Let me tell you why.

My early years are filled with contrasting memories of feeling loved as well as insecure. I grew up in an itty bitty 400 square feet home in a medium-sized town in north-central India. I was raised by kind and loving parents who raised me with good values and modeled 'those values. But unknown to them, I was about seven when a bully hammered into my head that I didn't belong to my family. He had me believe that I was picked up from the street. And I believed him. I spent a proportion of my childhood feeling insecure and vulnerable, worried that I will be discovered and taken back to where I rightly belonged.

As things became better, at about age 14, I developed a neurological illness. I would become unconscious without any warning and had to be on multiple medications that would make me dizzy and drowsy for most of the day. Nevertheless, with the support of my family I worked hard, that's all I could do, and at age 17 entered med school in my home town of Bhopal, India. Just as life was beginning to settle, within a few months of starting the med school, we experienced one of the worst industrial disasters of all time in my home town.

On December 2nd of that year, we were woken up at 2 AM with loud banging on the door. I saw a sea of humanity running in one direction, up the hill, fleeing deadly methyl isocyanate (MIC), that had leaked from a factory. We ran for our dear life. We survived. Two days later I showed up at the hospital door to see how I could help. As a first-year medical student, there was little tangible I could do, but I saw stuff that a 17-year-old should not be seeing. Things didn't get a whole lot better over the next several years. So, by the time I was preparing to come to the U.S., I thought I would find this to be one big Disneyland. I thought people here grow up as a child playing in Disneyland, when adults they play slots in Las Vegas, and they retire in Florida playing bingo. Decidedly, I had seen too many movies.

My perspective in 1994

But the truth as you can imagine was very different. Overall, **about a third of us are getting by just fine, a third struggling, and a third extremely stressed**. I believe, even these numbers may be underestimating the struggle. Those hurting are sometimes not even aware they are hurting as much, and many suffer in silence.

Not a week goes by when I don't hear about someone burnt out or who hurt himself or herself because of toxic stress. That doesn't make sense. **People don't work hard in school and college and go to work only to become disengaged, burnt out or much worse, take their lives.** "Something is going on here that I need to understand from a more in-depth perspective," I thought.

I came to become an oncologist but thought that searching for the reasons why well-meaning people, many of them extraordinarily brilliant and successful, struggle, and finding ways to help them will be worthwhile. I read tens of thousands of research studies, traveled different parts of the world, met sages, scientists and philosophers. I put all my learning on paper and found several different paths, all worthy and meaningful, toward thriving. But pretty quickly the concepts became complex and cumbersome. I show you one such model in the accompany figure.

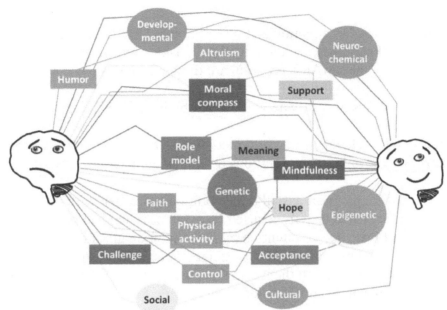

The Complex Path to Resilience

To simplify the ideas, I did the best thing I could—I started thinking deeper. After what seemed like a million years of thinking, slowly a theme began to develop. Next, I summarize the core idea in two simple formulas.

The Two Formulas
Here are the two simple formulas that summarize it all:

#1. *Life = n*experiences (L=n*E)*
Life is a series of experiences. If you add all your experiences that becomes your life.

#2. *Experience = Attention + Interpretation (E=A+I)*

Every experience has two components—attention & interpretation (think about the experience of seeing an apple. You first get its information by attention, and then interpret that information based on what you already know)

If I can influence my attention and interpretations, I can change my experiences, I surmised, which in turn can change my life. The three components of the SMART program are drawn from this basic idea:

Awareness—This is mostly about how our brain operates, and our neural vulnerabilities
Attention—Developing deep, sustained, focused, and intentional attention
Attitude—Cultivating interpretations driven by core values

Each part of the program has all three components, albeit with different emphasis. Part 1 was heavily focused on awareness and had practices geared to cultivate deeper attention by focusing it on gratitude. In part 2 now we will find moments when we guide our attention externally, focusing more in-depth on the world that surrounds us. Sometimes I call it the SOY approach (Search Outside Yourself)!

Here are some images/events I never get tired of watching—fall colors, sunrise, sunset, puppies playing, Halloween costumes, children's eyes, an airplane taking off or landing, penguins waddling, baby elephant's swaying trunk, our beautiful blue planet earth looked at from a distance. The above is only a partial list. The full list could fill at least a few pages. Not savoring at least one of these sensory treats during a day makes for an incomplete day. Mindful presence completes my day. So, what is mindful presence?

Presence is your conscious experience at this moment. Your experience can be an automatic flow of wandering attention or be a directed, intentional presence. The former is our default state; the latter is mindful presence (Intentional, focused, deep). Mindful presence has two parts based on where you are focusing—with the senses focusing on the external world (mindful noticing); with the mind focusing on inner thoughts and feelings (mindful thinking).

With mindful noticing, you exercise greater choice in what fills your sensory experience just as you choose what you are going to eat at a restaurant. You don't tell the server to get whatever. You pick the food that agrees with your appetite and palate.

When mindfully thinking you choose your thoughts instead of letting thinking happen to you. You choose thoughts that are deeper and prioritize kindness. Continuing the restaurant metaphor, if we leave our brain alone to do its thinking, it will tell the server, "Can you get me some stale thoughts please, thoughts that'll make me feel unhappy tomorrow?" Hence the importance of choosing your thoughts—intentional, deeper, kinder.

Left to itself, the human brain generates unhealthy, negative, "yucky" thoughts.

In general, I have found that **it is easier to train our attention by focusing it on the sensory world than by directing it inward**. Hence, we start our training in mindful presence with first focusing on the outside world. Let's start by reviewing how and what our brain attends.

14. The Mindless Brain (In Colors)

Experiencing the intricacies of biology for me is as fascinating as learning about the transformation of a caterpillar into a butterfly for a second grader. As a medical student, the first magical tool I got was a stethoscope. It opened me to the orchestra that plays in our body 24x7— of heartbeats, lung sounds, intestinal gurgles, and more. Next, I trained myself in ultrasound (called echocardiography) of the heart. Watching the heart valves doing purposeful Zumba regulating the blood flow into and out of the four chambers, all immersed in a well-choreographed activity carried out in precision about one hundred thousand times every day, was truly fascinating. Then my heart truly skipped a beat when 14 years ago, my wife and I saw the flicker of the heartbeats of our elder daughter, Gauri. That heart sure seemed in a hurry. It had so much to accomplish in the next few months. Seeing and hearing biology in action is a spiritual experience.

More recently, I was amazed to watch different brain areas dancing in real time—seeing thoughts moving like waves in the brain. A person sat in the MRI machine with his eyes closed, thinking, as the change in blood flow across his brain was mapped. The resulting movie, that I love to show as often as I can, displays how his thought train runs from one station to another. As he sat in the machine mind wandering, different parts of the brain turned red together, that roughly meant they were collaborating, hosting a particular thought. I tease him at one specific time he must have gotten furious, perhaps thinking about his

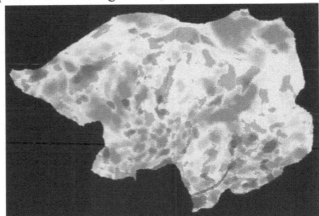

A still from the dancing brain video

neighbor's dog barking at night, when his entire brain turned red.

Senses or Thoughts

At any moment your attention can be either with your sensory system or your thoughts. When with the sensory system you are generally focused on the external world. **The senses engage with what is interesting (novel), pleasant, or painful, preferably the former two.** Perhaps you haven't paid much attention to your kitchen sink, bedroom window or office furniture in a while. But you immediately start noticing if you go to watch a new construction in the parade of homes, or if you get the corner office with a window.

Our physical body typically draws attention when it is hurting. Further, we are often judgmental about our body. Seldom do we look at our reflection and say, "Look at that lovely face." We want to be different than we are. Our 14-year-old with curly hair wants to make her hair straight; our 8-year-old with straight hair wants perms.

The second domain of attention is with your thoughts. We have two kinds of thoughts—intentional (the ones you choose) and automatic. We choose our thoughts before an important meeting, when negotiating with a grumpy relative, or when deciding what to tell the insurance staff, so they approve our claim. Most of the day, however, automatic thinking related to all the undone tasks, concerns, fears, hurts, and regrets, creates a background static to our activities.

Until recently for our species, most of our time was spent with these two domains. Of late, we have created a third domain that engages our attention and has very quickly come to dominate our day.

The Third Domain

The third domain is one of the smartphones (and screens in general). Let's talk about this for a bit. Today, **an average person checks his or her smartphone about 80 times a day**—once every 12-15 minutes.

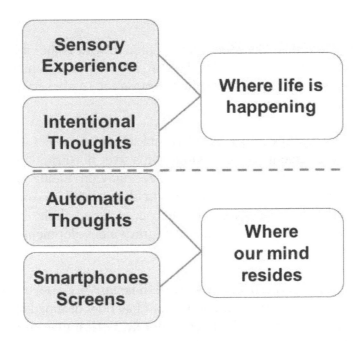

Our attention wastes inordinate amount of time disconnected from the real world

You might have seen people walking like praying mantis, holding their phones. It is so difficult to keep an elevator conversation. Parking lots and road crossings have become treacherous places with people walking with their heads buried. In one study **one out of three persons crossed the road distracted by cell phone.**

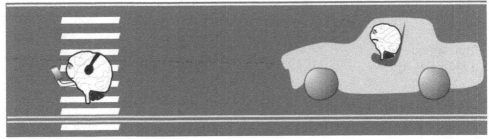

We risk our lives mindlessly scrolling through our screens

While driving, I almost always run into someone who is looking at his or her Smartphone, often at the traffic light. A 2015 report estimated that 660,000 drivers are distracted by cellphones on the road every day. That number is likely higher now.

When attending to our devices, we start making poor choices—sedentary lifestyle over movement, virtual relationships over nurturing connections, screening for information over deeper reflection. Convincing research shows that **excessive screen time has several unhealthy associations**: inactivity, weight gain, higher blood glucose, elevated cholesterol, sleep disruption, poorer mental health, lower cognitive development, and worse relationships.

Work performance and productivity are also negatively affected. One study showed that the human attention span has now dropped to about nine seconds, worse than goldfish. **Internet addiction presently has a global prevalence of over six percent** and is sure to rise in the coming decades.

I saw an interesting story recently when a man came out of jail after about 45 years of incarceration. He noted that when he was imprisoned people talked to each other, walked looking up, and very few people worked for the FBI (walking with a walkie-

Interesting! Everyone now works for the FBI.

What a person who came out of jail (after about 45 years) thought when he saw the way people walk today

talkie). Now we are mostly silent, looking downward as we walk, and he thought, everyone works for the FBI (wearing headphones).

Social media was designed to connect us; it is increasing our loneliness. Smartphones have become our surrogate body parts. They welcome us in the morning and are the last to bid us goodnight. From the first introduction of iPhones in 2007, how have Smartphones taken over the world so fast?

The answer is simple. **We are by design curious hunters and gatherers.** We used to collect food, but now we gather information. Smartphones and social media appeal to our curiosity instinct. Each future version of social media/websites/gadgets is pulling us deeper into the virtual world. Being informed isn't bad, but beyond a limit, greater information provides little additional utility. It only increases our anxiety and comes at a hefty cost—stealing our time away from deeper thoughts, experiences, and connections. As a result, we spend the bulk of the day in automatic thinking or with the screens, while life is happening elsewhere.

Automatic thinking and screens keep our attention weak and superficial. **Training attention entails pulling it out of the domains that weaken it, into areas that will make it stronger, deeper, and focused— intentional thoughts and the outside world.** We already started with intentional thinking with the morning gratitude practice. We will come back to it in part 4, resilient mindset. Presently, our focus will be to bring attention to the outside world with some of the specific ideas and practices that follow.

Our world has two parts: people & everything else. The practice with people is the 'two-minute rule' and with everything else is the 'curious moments.'

15. The Two-Minute Rule

Allow me to pry into your personal life for a second. Think about the answer to these two questions:

1. Have you recently paid attention, even for just two seconds, at the color of your loved one's eyes? (If you live alone, you can swap loved one for a friend, a colleague, a neighbor, a pet, or someone else you like.)

2. Do you know if the screws (on the electrical sockets) in your living room are aligned horizontal, vertical, or in some other direction?

If you aren't sure when was the last time you noticed your loved one's (or friend's) eyes, then you might enjoy the two-minute rule idea. If you feel you don't see the world around you as much, then the curious moments practice I share in the next chapter will be worth trying. Let's talk about the two-minute rule first.

The two-minute rule is fairly straightforward: **Give two minutes of undivided attention to at least one person every day who deserves that attention but isn't presently getting it.** We will start this practice with your family, perhaps your spouse or children and share it in the context of a family of four, and then extend to professional colleagues, customers, and others.

Core practice #2: Give two minutes of undivided attention to at least one person each day who deserves that attention but isn't presently getting it.

The Two-Minute Rule at Home: Background

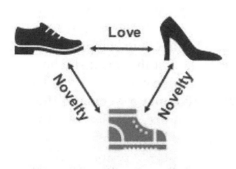

Novelty often beats love in pulling our attention

Imagine this scenario. You are visiting your local mall and sitting in a coffee shop with your spouse/partner. A few minutes later you see your high school buddy. You haven't met him or her for twenty years. Who will be more interesting for the next two minutes— your spouse/partner or high school buddy? The answer is obvious. No need to feel guilty if it's the high school buddy; I have asked this question over 5,000 times, and every single person responds with the high school buddy. Why is that?

It's because the primary connection between you and your spouse is of love, while that between you and high school buddy is of novelty. **The way the human brain operates, novelty beats love almost all the time.**

I recently asked my wife her first thought when she sees me at the end of the workday. She looked at me long and hard, and her answer was—"What chores can I get you to do today." We had a good laugh. That's not how we started, but after a few decades of being together, unless we actively seek and create novelty in our relationships, loved ones can become borderline boring.

My wife's "self-confessed" first thought when we meet at the end of the day!

Here is the price we pay for this change. Do you want to guess for how long is a family together at the end of an average day? Half an hour, fifteen minutes, five minutes? The correct answer according to a study is 90 seconds. That's all. And even when we are physically present, we are not mentally present. We are most likely thinking about uncompleted work, a phenomenon called the Zeigarnik effect, after the scientist who described it in the 1920s. The ten-hour workday often ends with thinking about work for another three hours. **We work 50 hours a week and then think about work for another fifteen hours or more.** It is the latter that gets us, because the whole week then becomes one big blob of work, with no opportunity for renewal. We give our brain no time to restore itself. Would you do that to your car engine or an electric mixer? I share this because you have an alternative that will need only two minutes of your time.

The Two-Minute Rule at Home: Practice

Let's say you were away for a business trip and hadn't met your family for a month. Will you find them more interesting after that gap? Most people say yes to that question. "There is more stuff to share." "I forget why I was angry with them." "They look more attractive after that gap." These are some of the comments I hear. So here is the practice:

I'm going to meet some very special people who I haven't seen in a long time.

For the past ten years, this is how I prepare myself before meeting my family

Meet your loved ones for the first two minutes at the end of each day as if you haven't seen them for thirty days. In essence, find novelty where love is. Here is how I do it.

At the end of the workday, when I start traveling back home, I pay more attention to the world around me to get out of my default mode. Sometimes I keep a theme—like I will notice the reds more today. In the garage, I check my emails. Next, I tell myself, "I'm going to meet some very special people who I haven't seen in a long time." With this intention, I go inside and try to notice novelty.

The first 30 seconds are crucial. **Over 75 percent of the connection happens in the first 30 seconds.** Here are two key parts to my practice that I suggest:

#1. Look at the color of their eyes—Within the first 30 seconds of arriving at home notice the color of your loved one's eyes. Do this only for two seconds otherwise you will freak them out! Your focus on noticing their eyes will make sure you come in their physical proximity, face them, and engage. Our eyes are special. They are the most expressive part of the face, a window into the brain, the heart, indeed the soul. When you pause and look at the color of your loved one's eyes, you experience a surge in oxytocin hormone—a hormone of connection, bonding, and trust. This phenomenon happens across species—when we look at puppies, we experience a rise in oxytocin, as do the puppies. Couples who are closer more often glance at each other's eyes. The opposite will likely work too—**lovingly gazing into each other's eyes will bring you closer**.

#2. Remind them that you care about them—When you meet someone after a gap of eight hours, they have no way to predict your mood. Will you be happy, annoyed, sad, reactive, calm? They spend considerable emotional energy in gauging who they are meeting. Best to remove that guesswork by reminding them you care about them as much or more than the last time you were with them. I find the following approaches helpful: tell them they were in your thoughts when you were away (I was thinking about what you said…, The purple flower reminded me of your…); remind them how they were right (Honey, you were right when you…); pay undivided attention (drop everything for two minutes and share a minute or two of non-judgmental time together).

There are countless ways to bring this idea to life. Here are a few things you can try: pack yourself with engaging information—a thought-provoking story, something interesting you saw; take a small gift, a favorite food item, or something else that might be interesting to them; play goofy (I have tied balloons to my eyeglasses, worn fire fighter's hat while walking in, pulled a stuffed toy from my jacket.)

The key is to let them know you are in a good mood (assuming you are). I want my children to find me cool and my wife to find me kind— predictably kind. Fascinating research shows that **when you are happy and express your cheerfulness to others, you not only improve their happiness but also enhance their physical health.**

I can attest that, compared to ten years ago, our every evening goes much better because of this conviction—finding novelty where your love is, deepens the love.

If I am not in a good mood: Not every day do I arrive home feeling cheerful. In most situations, however, spreading the negativity won't help. **Nasty managers increase the risk of divorce among employees and lower their kids' grades in the school.** We shouldn't give that power to anyone.

Block the negativity at your level. Here are four things I try on a day I don't have the right pep while getting inside the home:

#1. Remind myself of gratitude—Remembering the reasons I am grateful to the people I will be meeting helps me be more intentional. It certainly helps put the conflicts in the background.

#2. Narrow my presence to this day—Sometimes **it helps to remember that this is the day I have got.** Tomorrow isn't a guarantee. Best to strive and make the most of this day. This awareness works like magic in focusing my attention to the positive and uplifting aspects of the day.

#3. Remind myself of the personal golden rule—My personal golden rule has six words: **"I am enough. I have enough."** This reminder pulls me out of my instinctive state of seeking. Research shows the bulk of our day is spent seeking one thing or another. Only when we stop seeking is our mind available to heal—the self and others.

#4. Remind myself of transience—I remind myself that I have 1200 days left before my teenager is off to college. Even with my second grader, I have 3500 days left before she is off to college too. I don't stew on this fact but get inspired by it. This reminder helps take away my focus from the negativity and direct my attention to what is in front of me.

**Reminding myself of transience
pulls me out of my attention sumps**

When you are the host: At my end, when I am home, and I hear the garage door open, I drop everything and meet my family in the garage. Earlier I used to greet them with my head buried into the computer. But now I close the screen and welcome them with full presence.

Even a simple thing as giving a glass of water to someone who is coming home at the end of a long day, or taking their bag or coat, can help them feel welcome, and change the flavor of the evening.

Here is what I have learned. **First impressions are very quick to form, within seconds or milliseconds, and stick for a long time.** We are making these first impressions all-day long. Also, even for someone familiar, if you are meeting them after a gap of eight hours, it is like you are meeting a new person as far as first impressions are concerned. So, **handle the first few moments of meeting someone with as much positive healing energy as you can bring**. Assume you are meeting a new person even if it is someone familiar. Help them laugh/feel worthy/or at least show you are in a good mood. Create a ritual together—a cup of coffee, a glass of water, a healthy snack together—whatever works for you. **Let them associate you with oxytocin and endorphins, not adrenaline and steroids.** Engaging with an authentic positive presence is an instinct we had as a two-year-old and dogs preserve into their old age. We can choose to rekindle this instinct.

The connection of the first few seconds will power the rest of your time together. So, light up in this time. (While teaching a workshop in Ireland, I once received a message that light up in Europe means smoking a cigarette. That's certainly not what I mean by light up!).

You have a choice: Handle the first two minutes well and set the tone for your entire evening; mess up those moments, and you are busy recovering the rest of the time. One of the ways to handle the two minutes well is to show your funny bone at this time.

Show Your Funny Bone

Humor is extraordinarily essential for your wellbeing. When you laugh with others, you signal that you are willing to play with them. **Laughter is less about something being funny and more about social connection.** Only 10-15% of the comments that evoke laughter are independently amusing. **The people we laugh with begin to like and trust us.**

Laughter is wonderfully healing for your body. Laughter releases healthy endorphins, relaxes the body, improves immunity, lowers blood pressure, and decreases pain. Researchers have found positive effects of laughter on stress, anxiety, depression, fatigue, sleep quality, respiratory function, and blood glucose.

Pick one or two good stories with appropriate humor and serve them to lift everyone's mood. If you aren't sure who to make fun of, direct it to yourself. Humor is most natural with little children. Even if your humor is childlike, adults will relish such humor, when you direct it toward children. **Your playfulness shows your emotional maturity.**

Remember that when you are happy and show it, you improve not only others' mood, but also their physical health. Also, laughter isn't about being funny; it is about connection. Further, **your happiness travels farther than the person immediately in front of you.** When you are happy, your friend is happy, friend's friend is happy, and friend's friend's friend is happy. That's a good reason to smile in this moment.

Your Happiness Travels to Three Degrees of Separation

The Two-Minute Rule at Home: Avoid this Trap

For loved ones, we have a learned behavior that hampers meaningful connections. It is the trap of our desire to improve them—all the time. The more they resist being improved, the greater our efforts to improve them. The resulting back and forth leads to unhealthy dynamics, where children associate their parents with feeling bad about themselves. The same happens to partners and other relationships.

With this dynamic developed, you both stop enjoying each other's company. You do not blossom in mutual presence, no longer are OK with being vulnerable, and communication channels dry up. A relationship that is missing healthy communication and where you can't share your vulnerability and feel judged won't be fun.

Here is what I suggest—**For the first two minutes you meet your loved ones, do not try to improve anyone at that time.** You will have opportunities for improvement later but resist that urge in the first two minutes. Once they start trusting that you won't be an emotional predator each time you meet them, an oxytocin bond will develop. Very likely, they will be much more amenable to critical feedback after some time.

One challenge you will face is that while you are ready to practice the two-minute rule, others might be stuck in their habitual mind wandering, catastrophizing, and negativity bias. You will have to **be patient and trust that your positivity and good intentions are ultimately infectious.** If your kids aren't joining, then practice this just with your spouse, best friend, neighbor, or someone else. **People like to be where a party is happening.** So, if your presence becomes an indication of joyous moments, they will ultimately clamor to be with you.

The goal is not to shock and awe them. The idea is to transcend our brain's instinctive wandering attention and negativity bias, so you spend a higher proportion of the time in affiliative connection.

Keep in mind that **a known side effect of the two-minute rule is an initial growing suspicion among your loved ones that you are up to something, that you have an agenda.** If they ask, you can let them know what you are doing. They will gradually come to recognize and trust your good

When you suddenly become kind, others suspect you have a hidden agenda

intentions.

The Two-Minute Rule at Work

The two-minute rule at work has three aspects.

First, you have a choice in how best to spread positivity. Either you can genuinely like others, or you can try and fake your appreciation. **The most natural approach is to genuinely like others.** Faking that feeling and expression will fatigue your facial muscles and your mind.

A few perspectives that will help you genuinely like others are: see them in their fuller social context (as a family member, friend, and more); understand, and in some instances assume, that they have several constraints and struggles; be grateful for their presence in your life; focus on what is right about them and less on what you find annoying.

Second, **minimize judgments in the first few minutes of meeting anyone.** Our instinct is to judge others' attractiveness, competence, and trustworthiness in less than half a second (more on this in Part 3). In this default state, we are busy all-day long judging everyone we are meeting. Also, when we judge others, we also feel judged by them. Best to exit this state and swap it with what follows as the next (third) aspect of the two-minute rule.

Third, in those two minutes help them feel worthy. Answer this question: "How often do you struggle with the feeling that you are appreciated too much at work?" I have asked this question to tens of thousands of employees and haven't ever had anyone responding in the affirmative.

So, it will be fair to **assume that every person you have ever met and will be meeting struggles with self-worth.** This awareness will help enhance most of your meetings and relationships. You can help others feel worthy in multiple ways, some more direct than others—giving undistracted attention, gifting appropriate praise, asking them about something they enjoy sharing, telling something about you that might bring the two of you closer to each other, mentioning a detail that shows you remembered them in their absence. A few supportive ideas are to sport a genuine smile, lean forward, shake hands with warmth, introduce yourself, and show you are in a good mood and very happy to meet them. Receiving such attention is enjoyable; giving such attention is doubly pleasing. What I have shared is just the starter kit. You can develop your ideas as you refine your interpersonal skills.

No one struggles with being appreciated too much. Most of us have many roles—parent, partner, professional, son/daughter, friend, neighbor. On most days, all of these roles demand our attention. With time being a zero-sum game, we are bound to come short in some aspect of life. Here is how it hurts us. **We anchor our self-worth in the domains where we are performing the worst.** We don't prioritize self-kindness or self-acceptance. This is particularly difficult for women given they still shoulder the bulk of the load of running their home and child care, in addition to professional work.

The example above is unreal. Most people do not struggle with being appreciated too much.

My wife, who is an excellent physician, mom, spouse, daughter, chef, and more, tries her best to give her 100 percent to each role. She cannot be at two places at the same time. She holds herself to standards that are impossible to meet. Of late, she is trying self-compassion and self-acceptance, but her basic tendency is to self-blame. I am sure many of you have a similar personal story.

Just assume the person in front of you has struggles, more than you know or can think of (more on this in the next section).

One realization that has helped me a lot is that **it is difficult to dislike someone you know likes you.** If you can genuinely help others believe that you adore and respect them, then despite the disagreements, they will still find it hard to dislike you.

The two-minute rule is a very effective way to sprinkle RUM moments during a busy day. **We experience most of our professional and personal time in three flavors: Adversarial, Transactional, and Affiliative.** Adversarial is obvious. Transactional interaction follows the business norm—"Honey how was your day? What's up for dinner?" Back to back questions offer no space for an authentic response to the first question.

Affiliative interaction takes a bit more time. The two-minute rule is a perfect of example of an approach that converts transactional encounters into affiliative ones. Even one such encounter during the day can lift your entire day.

The next practice, curious moments, helps connect you more in-depth with the world that surrounds you—through cultivating a sense of curiosity.

16. Curious Moments

Won't it be nice if your brain was younger five years from now than it is today? Let's see how we can do that.

The Happiest Bunch

We are the happiest as a young kid. Then teenage conflicts take over, followed by college pressures, new relationships, work commitments, and more. Only in the later years of our life do we claim back our happiness, when wisdom arrives, our priorities and meaning become more explicit, and we stop fighting ourselves.

The kids are the happiest partly because of their curiosity, often defined as their love of learning. Spend a few minutes with a two-year-old, and you will agree with me. Kids naturally seek novelty and fun and can create joy out of the most mundane of objects and activities. A balloon can become a soccer ball, a coloring board, or a punching bag. Their gift in finding novelty in the mundane comes from their flexibility in interpretations.

Recall the two ingredients of an experience—attention (A) and interpretation (I)—that we discussed in chapter 13. **The ratio of attention and interpretation colors your experience.** Attention brings you the information that you then interpret based on your fund of knowledge. As a child with less fund of knowledge, attention dominates our

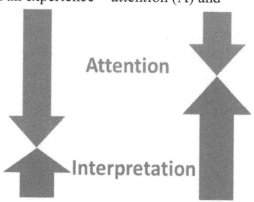

AI Ratio (Attention Interpretation Ratio) in childhood (left) and older age (right)

experience. As things become familiar, interpretations begin to dominate our experience, until we reach a point where we barely attend.

For example, imagine looking at a rainbow. In the figure, the downward pointing arrow shows attention, while the upward pointing arrow shows interpretations. The pair of arrows on the left shows a child looking at a rainbow for the first time—with deep attention. On the right is a grownup who has seen rainbows a million times looking at it now, with little attention and strong interpretations.

In general, **we find greater joy in experiences that keep our attention for a longer period.** Unfortunately, attrition in attention and domination of interpretations is a natural consequence of aging. With prior experience, we have pre-imagined constructs, biases, and strong preferences—all of these interfere with an authentic experience.

For grownups, the primary source of joy switches from novelty to meaning. Kids are happy discovering novel things; adults are gladly doing meaningful things. Won't it be nice though if we experienced a little more novelty while pursuing meaning? Let's give it a try by awakening our curiosity.

Research shows that **the more curious you are, the better your memory in your senior years and the longer your lifespan.** While I cannot promise it with the full backing of science, I can say that one of the ways to keep your brain agile and young is to remain curious. The key aspect of this change is to increase the AI ratio in your experience, by deepening and sustaining your attention.

A Curious Moment
Pick a flower, any flower. If you can't find one around you, search for "yellow daisy" on the internet. Pull one image and try to notice these five details in this daisy:

1. The number of layers of petals
2. The jagged edges of the petals (and how each jagged edge is unique)
3. Two or three lines on the surface of the petals that break them into segments
4. The intricate pattern of the central stamen
5. Color pattern of the petals from central to periphery

The purpose of this activity is not to look at *a* daisy, but to look at *this* daisy, in all its uniqueness. A practice like this deepens your attention, even if for a brief moment. It also helps you get to know this particular daisy how it looks today. With repetition, this practice makes your attention stronger for a brief moment, helping you effortlessly be more intentional, with fewer mind wanderings. With constancy of practice, you can experience a lasting change in attention.

I was working on a project while traveling to San Diego. From Rochester, MN to San Diego, CA, a distance of about 2000 miles, I changed two flights over six hours, walked past a few thousand people at the airport, but barely noticed anything. I was mostly working on my laptop, writing a research proposal, or thinking about the research plan. Do you think any human could have made a two-mile trip with such unawareness five hundred years ago? As hunter-gatherers we saw new vistas almost every day, bringing us novelty as well as unique threats, forcing us to attend to the world fully. While we cannot return to the same lifestyle, we have probably pushed to the other extreme and disengaged ourselves from the world just because we can afford to do it. Here is another small attention practice that will enhance your AI ratio.

Your Intricate Design

Pause your reading for a second and look at both your hands. Notice the size and shape of your fingers. Compare the ring and pointer fingers of the left hand. Which finger is longer? Next, compare the ring and pointer fingers of the right hand with each other. Which finger is longer? Are your two sides symmetric or do you have asymmetry in finger length?

Likely, you didn't know this detail about yourself. You have had your hands for a few decades. While this is a trivial little detail, noticing it is an early step toward you seeing more profound specifics about yourself, others, and the world around you.

Here is a little challenge. Look at the brain on your right. Study all the different lines inside this brain. Did you find the letter M?

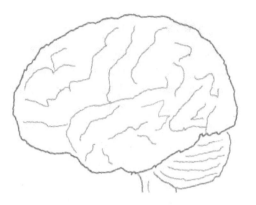

Now try to memorize these lines and draw the brain from your memory, first the outline and then the inside lines. Hint: work with remembering only one line at a time.

While boarding an airplane I often enjoy watching different hairstyles. Buzz cut, crew cut, side part, ponytail, layered, bob cut—I have seen them all. Every single person sports a unique hairstyle.

As you notice the details in the world and yourself, it is important to delay your judgments. Avoid adjectives such as good—bad, like it—don't like it, etc. **The moment we stamp an adjective, we stop attending.** Notice that I didn't say non-judgmental, I am only suggesting delayed judgment.

A question you might ask is, "If I delay assigning adjectives, am I not depriving myself of uplifting emotions?" It is a very reasonable concern. Interestingly, curiosity (and delayed-judgment noticing) by itself is a powerful source of positive emotions. Delaying judgment and deeper noticing will thus open up an independent source of positive emotions. Further, when you appreciate something after deeper learning, appreciation is stronger and longer lasting.

Curiosity with its attendant positive emotions places you into a self-feeding upward spiral. Here is how it works. When something novel appears in your sensory realm, you notice it more. This phenomenon works the other way too. **When you choose to see something more carefully, you start finding it novel.** Since this experience provides positive emotions, it leaves a more profound imprint and calls you to re-experience the same. You instinctively reengage your attention toward greater noticing, eventually cultivating a positive, uplifting habit.

FOND

The FOND acronym stands for Find One New Detail. A simple way to deploy deeper attention and kindle the curiosity instinct is to **find one new detail you hadn't noticed before**. It could be related to shape, sound, fragrance, feel, color—any detail you hadn't seen before of an object otherwise familiar. It could also be discovering an entirely new thing in a familiar environment.

Find a new detail in the ring you wear on your hands, the front page of this book, in the flowerpot in your garden, in the design of your dining table, in the branching pattern of trees, in the steps or the elevator that lead to your home. Notice a stump of an old tree in your neighborhood, a clock that has run out of battery in your home, the way the screws align on the electrical sockets in your home.

This habit of noticing details will sharpen your memory and can be critical to not getting lost in a new city or when hiking. You might also observe that when you get to know the objects around you a little more, you start getting fond of them.

Smart, Slow, Savor

Ever since we have learned to create processed and refined foods, we have taken away the connection between the amount we eat, and the calories consumed. Ten grams of butter has 70 calories, while ten grams of lettuce has less than two calories. If we don't make the right selections, in a few minutes, we can consume a few thousand calories without filling our quarter gallon stomach. What makes matters worse is that **it takes some time for the brain to know how many calories have moved from the plate to the mouth and landed in the stomach.**

Further, our eating speed has accelerated with the pace of life. Thus, we consume three slices of pizza—about 900 calories, in twenty bites. On a day we are hungry, the first bite will taste awesome. The second bite will taste awesome too. And then the next fifteen bites merge into an unfelt blob. We finally become aware again, at the last two bites. The result— we swallowed 900 calories without thoroughly enjoying it. We are then standing in front of the refrigerator, wondering what more we can eat.

Food gives two kinds of energy—the energy of the calories and the energy of the joy. If I don't get the joy energy, then even though I may have a full stomach, I am still mentally hungry.

I suggest an alternative. Just for today try eating with a more authentic presence. Three components of better eating are—Smart, Slow, Savor.

Smart: Pick healthier fresher options. I am sure you have heard of the obvious suggestions—avoid calorie-dense food, no trans-fat, etc. Here is a simple idea: **In each meal, keep at least one or two options that were alive in the last week (preferably plant based).**

Slow: I heard growing up that we should chew each bite 32 times, which is the number of teeth in our mouth. The digestive process starts in the mouth itself. By chewing slowly, you not only get more taste but also help your stomach.

Savor: Savor at least the first five bites by connecting your mind with the taste of the food. Try to carry as far as you can beyond the five bites. Notice the color, aroma and feel the texture of your food. Keep grateful thoughts for all those who made the meal possible for you—from the farmers to grocers and the preparers.

Look at eating as a daily celebratory spiritual practice, geared not just to feed calories to your body, but also to give joy to the mind, depth to the relationships, and a moment to pay gratitude to nature—the source of it all for us.

Mindful eating helps decrease caloric intake

Curious Living

As you sprinkle curiosity into your days, eventually you want curiosity to upgrade from a practice to becoming a way of life so you notice at least a few extra details than you would have otherwise and delay your judgment just a little bit more. Here are a few ideas I have personally implemented. I hope one or more of these will resonate with you.

- While reading a book to our then four-year-old, we would pause and notice details on the page. Like, how many monkeys have their mouths open, how many bugs have their eyes closed, can you count the number of beads in that bracelet, spy a small purple balloon, and so on. We would do the same with watching videos.

- While driving, we would often notice the design of ponytails of different cars (the antennas). Some are short, some long, some broad, some stiff, and some shake with the wind. We also went through the chimney phase where we would notice the designs of different chimneys on top of the houses.

- A few years ago, I started a practice with our then eight-year-old, where I would report to her one new thing I saw during the day, and she would do the same. The practice helped us find a topic to share and start a good conversation.

**Sharing novel details with children
is a great conversation starter**

- Being curious with the people you meet in a nonintrusive way is a great practice. **When you look at a cab driver, try to see a family of four. When you look at a grocery clerk, try to see a**

mother or father, brother or sister. When you look at a senior gentleman, try to see a grandfather or a war veteran. It will make you kinder.

- Consider taking a curiosity stroll for five minutes in the middle of the day. Start with telling yourself—no planning or problem solving during this time. Then take a stroll and try to notice at least one new detail that you hadn't noticed before. The first few times you do this practice, you will be surprised at some large objects you may have missed before. Walking is a bit like coffee for your brain. When you are feeling brain fatigue, take a curiosity stroll at your workplace before you go for a cookie. **Taking a walk increases energy supply for the brain and freshens you.**

- Access your photostream every so often. When flying, I see people playing silly games on their phones, quietly staring into space, chatting, or viewing videos, sometimes toxic looking videos. Seldom I see anyone looking at old family pictures.

  According to one estimate, we took 105 billion digital photos in 2015 in the US alone (about one photo per day per person). Another estimate is one trillion the world over. You likely have hundreds if not thousands of interesting pictures and videos stored in your smartphone. Why not spend some time together as a family watching old pictures/videos, particularly of little children. We naturally affiliate with children. The innocence of kids awakens the loving, compassionate being within us. **When you see your spouse, sibling or parent as a child, you will see the softer more vulnerable part of them. It will bring you closer.**

- Engage non-visual senses as much as you can. Each experience is a multisensory phenomenon created by integration of our senses. However, vision dominates for most of us. Interestingly, when vision clashes with sound, vision alters what we hear. Similarly, vision changes what we taste. Our instinct is to trust vision the most. However, our vision can be biased based on our preference. **Often, we order eyes to see what we prefer to find, not how it is**—an observation that has made us question the reliability of eyewitness testimony. The more you can engage touch, hearing, and smell, the richer will be your sensory experience.

- An interesting way to engage touch and hearing is to feel your own body. Gently tap your forehead, your scalp, your cheek, your thigh, your belly, and your chest wall. Notice different sounds. Physicians call this percussion and can diagnose various medical conditions with just the sound they hear.

I will repeat here what I said earlier. **If you wish for your brain to be younger five years from now than it is today, cultivate greater curiosity.** Get in the habit of more intentional seeing, listening, smelling, tasting, and hearing. Delay judgment, live deeper, and become a student of the world around you. You will realize that curiosity will not only enrich your life, it will also foster greater creativity, more joy, and deeper relationships.

17. Summary

As a reminder, the two core practices from module I and II are noted below. Integrate these well in your life before proceeding to add a third practice from module III.

> **Core practice #1: First thing in the morning, think about five people in your life who mean a lot to you and send them your silent gratitude.**

> **Core practice #2: Give two minutes of undivided attention to at least one person each day who deserves that attention but isn't presently getting it.**

The two main points from module II that I wish to recap before moving to module III are:
1. Mindful presence is an intentional presence
2. Novelty and meaning are the two primary sources of resilience/joy

Mindful Presence is an Intentional Presence

Presence is your conscious experience at this moment, which can be automatic or intentional. Automatic presence is our default. Mindful presence is an intentional presence. Just as you choose what you eat at a restaurant (and do not let the server decide your options), **with mindful presence, you decide where and to what depth you deploy your attention.**

With stronger and more intentional attention, as you become better aware of what you are thinking (called meta-awareness), it doesn't matter whether your presence is in the past, the present, or the future because all-day long you are driven by values and meaning. **Eventually, intentional**

kind presence becomes your default. That's when you have transformed.

Mindful presence thus isn't being in the present moment. Nor it is emptying the mind. **The mind wasn't created to be emptied just as the heart wasn't built to be stopped.** Emptying the mind isn't possible or desirable. What we need is to have a better influence on the content and flow of our thoughts. Instead of draining the mind, fill it with nurturing sensory experiences, creative ideas, uplifting emotions, and motivation. Bring courage, hope, and inspiration to your mind. Fill it with gratitude and compassion. That I believe will provide a lasting and transformative benefit.

As the animal brains evolved, they developed complex structure enabling our capacity to think, imagine, plan, prioritize, and mentally time travel. This ability has helped us create a beautiful world. It has created problems too, including the fear of the future and regrets of the past. Given that our brain has structurally changed, forcing the mind to the confines of the present moment is like confining a hummingbird to just one branch of a tree. It will neither work, nor is desirable. **Any species that has imagination and preferences and has to take care of babies can't be in the present.** A better alternative is to be intentional about what fills the present.

With intentionality, you become flexible about your perspective. If the intermediate or long term seems challenging, you can zoom in and think of the very short term. For example, if you are due for a colonoscopy two weeks from now, you can choose to live one day at a time, instead of thinking about the prep and all that. If you feel challenged in the short term, such as in the middle of an unpleasant dental procedure, you can choose to zoom out and think about the weekend plans.

Such a perspective helps you develop a healthier relationship with time. It gives you freedom from being bound by time.

So, I believe it is better to define your presence by intentionality and not so much by time. Remember that most animals are in the present moment yet haven't become self-actualized. I believe our ability to harness our imaginations by becoming intentional will provide a more robust and pragmatic long-term solution.

Novelty and Meaning are the Two Core Sources of Resilience/Joy

I once heard an adorable expression. It was something like this. "Mom is away for the weekend. Cindy, Sarah, Crystal and Mike are alone at home with their Dad." While it is lovely for them to be missing their mom, finding novelty in each other might be an excellent long-term investment!

An interesting neighbor who is full of great stories is much more engaging than a boring close relative. It is part of our biological design— to focus on novelty. Some phone calls you readily pick, others you prefer sending to the answering machine. The second group of people are either trying to sell you something you don't want to buy, are strangers, or are familiar but boring. **Our brain finds boring people dreadful. Equally dreadful is the fact that those dearest to us can become boring with time.** Once they are away or gone, we miss them and feel guilty. Hence the need to meet them as if you haven't seen them for a long time, focusing on and finding their novelty.

Complement this with delaying the urge to improve others, so they associate you with feeling good about themselves. In this time help them feel worthy, share a good story, and show you are in a good mood. Similar to people, **when you start finding novelty in the world around you, you become better connected with the world.** You become a student again. Your backyard or kitchen will become a more interesting site, as will the vegetables or fruit section in your grocery store.

You will be living in the real world, not in your head. You might also notice that you start getting new ideas and become more creative at your workplace. Also, you become kinder, to others and yourself.

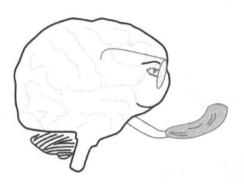

He seems to have mastered the art of non-judgmental noticing. He spends more time studying the cucumber than eating it.

Let's talk about compassion now, or its cousin, kindness. In the next module, we go still deeper and explore the single most desirable trait every person wants in their partner and friend—kindness.

MODULE III

Kindness

The third module, kindness, helps us understand and remove the barriers we face in cultivating kindness toward others and self.

18. The Mortar

A bricklayer knows that he can't just stack the bricks on top of another and hope they will withstand the elements. The bricks need mortar to stay together. Without mortar, they crumble, like the ones on the left in the figure below.

Bricks need mortar to stay together. That mortar in relationships is kindness.

That mortar in human relationships is kindness, the single most desirable trait in your partner. **Kindness is the glue that keeps together every brick of your life—family, friends, neighborhood, work.**

Unlike the mortar for the bricks, **the kindness mortar has to be built fresh every day.** You can't tell your loved ones, "I was kind yesterday, but today I am in no mood."

Kindness Isn't Optional

When it comes to interspecies competition or competition between two prides of lion or most animal groups, kindness has little role. But within most human units—a family, a tribe, an organization—kindness or its close cousin, collaboration and collegiality, are essential for thriving. Increasingly, the size of that unit is expanding because of our growing interdependence. A key factor here is the vulnerability of our very young.

Our children need collaboration among tens of thousands of people each day for their safety and success. If your child is in school, you depend on thousands of employees of the school district for your child's wellbeing— the teacher, the staff, the janitor, and others. When you seek help in a medical facility, a different universe attends to you. A very different universe greets you in the mall. All these worlds are interconnected. The energy, positive or negative, in one world diffuses to the other because it's the same people who traverse through these areas.

Kindness thus isn't optional. It is essential if we are to secure the safety of our children and the smooth running of our society. Why then is kindness sometimes not our default? For two reasons—one it takes effort and self-control to remain consistently kind, and two kindness is construed by some as weakness. Let's explore the second reason.

Kindness Isn't Weakness

I often show a picture of an athlete lifting two-hundred pounds and compare it with the 4'10" frame of Mother Teresa, and then ask—Who is stronger? The answer I universally get is Mother Teresa. We know that **the kindest among us are the strongest.**

Kindness is thus a marker of strength. The higher cortical brain (the prefrontal cortex) that hosts kindness is the key area humans have grown to distinguish ourselves from every other species on the planet. This area helps us focus, think deeper, think flexibly, connect the dots, negotiate complexity, have self-control, forgive, and exercise courage.

Kindness also does wonders to our immune system. The opposite of kindness—anger, hatred, and envy—inflame us, suppress our immune system, and predispose to autoimmunity. Kindness does the opposite, enhancing anti-inflammatory arm of our immune system and empowering our immune system to fight the external agents.

Kindness is the perfect flavor to choose when you are giving negative feedback or disciplining someone. A few years ago, as I was driving my daughter Gauri to her school, she shared with guilt in her voice that she forgot her lunch box at home. Now the choice was between turning around and getting late for the meeting by 30 minutes or a hungry kid by mid-afternoon. I chose the former. Just as I was about to give her negative feedback, I switched to kindness. I said, "I am so glad you forgot your lunch today." She waited for the cynical downpour. Instead of that, I said, "When was the last time we had an extra thirty minutes in the morning. Let's make the best of this time." We car-danced to home and back to school. She remembers that experience to this day and hasn't forgotten her lunch since. I believe the strength of kindness helped her change her behavior.

Can't Carry the Canoe

Just as kindness to others isn't our default, kindness to the self is also not our default. In my workshops, almost everybody responds yes to this question: Have you recently felt bad about yourself?

**The good among us are good
at feeling bad about themselves**

To some extent, self-judgment pushes us to work harder. Self-acceptance, taken to an extreme, can foster apathy and low standards. Most successful

123

people I have met aren't satisfied with the status quo and their accomplishments. As a result, we sometimes equate nurturing a state of dissatisfaction with being passionate. The question to ask is, will the skills and perspectives that have served you in the past continue to help you grow in the future? The example of the canoe is instructive.

Two men strive to reach a treasure up on a mountain. For that, they have to cross a river, walk on the land, and then climb the mountain. They each cross the river in a small canoe. Then they carry the canoe on their back, lest the canoe is stolen. Now, can they climb the mountain with the canoe on their back? The obvious answer is no.

I think we have to drop the canoe if we hope to climb the mountain.

In order to grow and ascend, sometimes we have to drop older ideas and pick up fresh new perspectives (self-kindness)

The canoe was essential to cross the river but is now a load. The same applies to some of our skills. **The skills that helped you reach so far may not be the skills that will help you climb higher. Perhaps self-judgment helped you come so far. But the next phase of your journey will need self-compassion.**

The single most important contributor to successful leadership is emotional intelligence. Emotional intelligence has four core components—Awareness of self + Awareness of others + Compassion toward self + Compassion toward others. Self-compassion thus is an essential ingredient of emotional intelligence, which in turn is key to your success at work, as well as in personal relationships.

One of the most significant impediments in compassion toward self and others is fear—fear that your compassion will be seen as weakness, fear that you won't have the energy to be authentically compassionate, and also the fear that your compassion will make you vulnerable.

The Fear of Becoming Vulnerable

On a trip to a theme park as we were waiting to ride on a bus, a little girl coming out of the bus started retching, threw up, and then fell. There was a mess everywhere. Everyone took a step back, fearful they might catch an infection from her.

Later that day as I thought about the group response, it was dominated by fear. The dark cloud of fear prevented the light of compassion. **Fear annihilates Compassion.** Fear creates distance. **Once fear invades our brain, most good thoughts escape.**

A particular challenge with fear is that given its focus on survival, **most cruel actions with fear as their basis, feel justified.** All pre-emptive strikes seem rational. **Fear expands our blind spot that hides our mistakes and our ignorance.**

The goal, however, isn't to demolish fear, which will be unreal and unachievable. Our goal is to keep our fear rational—the way we want the fire in the fireplace but want to keep it contained, so it only burns the wood in the fireplace, not the living-room sofa.

The fear in our brain is generated and contained by collaborative efforts of three lieutenants that we will talk about next. When collaborating smoothly, they help you take the optimal risk while keeping you safe. But when imbalanced, they can turbocharge fear, or in rare instances completely take the fear away—both undesirable and limiting.

19. The Three Lieutenants

Three brain areas (the three lieutenants) generate and regulate the fear response: the amygdala, the hippocampus, and the prefrontal cortex.

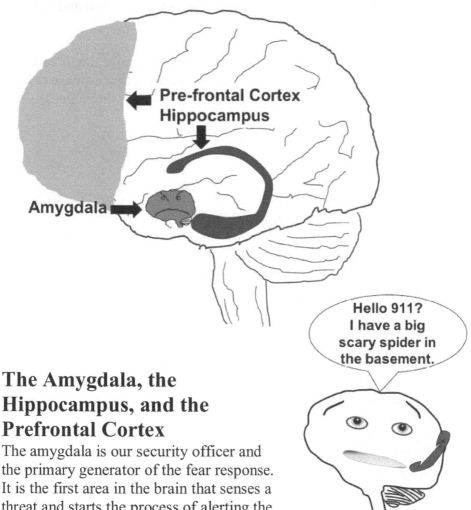

The Amygdala, the Hippocampus, and the Prefrontal Cortex

The amygdala is our security officer and the primary generator of the fear response. It is the first area in the brain that senses a threat and starts the process of alerting the rest of the brain to wake up and focus. **If you have an overactive amygdala, you'll generate an outsized reaction to a minor stressor.**

A Brain with Overactive Amygdala Overreacts to Minor Stressors

127

The two areas of the brain that mentor and restrain the amygdala are the hippocampus and the pre-frontal cortex. The hippocampus runs the memory orchestra, while at the same time keeping the amygdala response in check. **People with smaller hippocampus have a runaway stress reaction to a stressor.** The prefrontal cortex (PFC) is your central executive that helps you keep your sense of humor in inching traffic. PFC enables you to mentor the amygdala, so its efforts are rational and helpful, instead of catastrophizing.

When this system is humming to perfection, you recognize the threats right away and launch a measured response. You fade the response once the risk is over. I so wish this was always the case. The system goes wrong in two situations.

What Goes Wrong

Some of us are born with an overactive amygdala and an underactive hippocampus and PFC. This neural vulnerability could be genetic or relate to the toxic effect of early life stressors. These are the people predisposed to anxiety, depression, bipolar disorder, attention deficit, and burnout. **Recognize that most mental health issues are biologically predisposed.**

The system also backfires when it is overtaxed. Our stress pathways are deft at handling transient stresses. A gazelle spotting a lion makes a run. Once in the safe zone, the gazelle's stress pathways quickly return to normal. The gazelle doesn't develop post-traumatic stress disorder (PTSD), because the gazelle cannot think itself into stress. Not so with humans.

Many of our modern stressors are long lasting—financial, health, relationships, crime, legal, loneliness, corruption. Further, many of our stressors seed large attention sumps that generate reverberating thoughts, predisposing us to experience the stressor in imagination (like the gazelle thinking all day about the lion encounter). These thoughts keep our stress systems revved up.

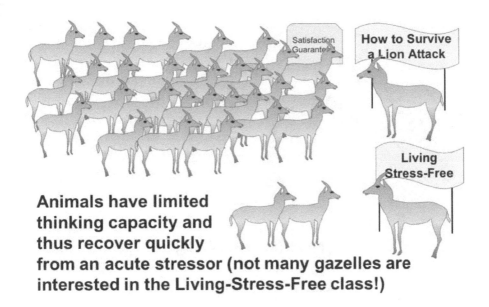

Animals have limited thinking capacity and thus recover quickly from an acute stressor (not many gazelles are interested in the Living-Stress-Free class!)

Our stress systems, however, weren't designed to tackle ongoing long-term stress. The pathways also materially change. Instead of hippocampus and PFC getting stronger with constant stress (like muscles would), they undergo atrophy. **With ongoing stress, the brain descends from thoughtful living to instinctive living.** Many of our body systems don't like this chronic instability, leading to high blood pressure, clogged arteries, inflammation, immune suppression, autoimmunity, predisposition to cancer, and more. What a design to maximize suffering and make us sick!

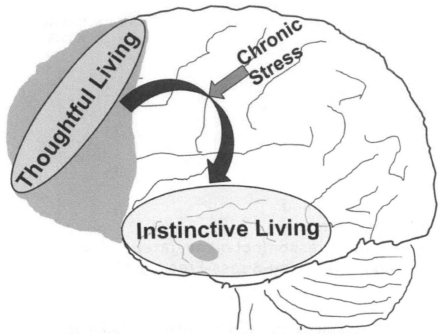

Chronic stress shifts the brain from thoughtful living to instinctive living

What We are Up Against

We are up against a system that isn't designed to provide lasting happiness. If you fall and have a small gash in the skin, the skin tries to heal. But by its negativity bias and overthinking, the mind keeps its wounds fresh. Let me repeat this: *The skin is designed to heal its wounds while the mind is designed to keep its wounds raw.* That's the challenge you face. How do you cure a wound that the body isn't trying to heal? That is the reason you have to take charge of your brain and change its thresholds.

We have to change the stress threshold, so little things don't bother us. We also have to develop ways to douse the stress response in time, so it doesn't smolder all-day long.

One way we can keep the stress response in check is through cultivating kindness. Kindness engages our higher cortical brain, shifting us from instinctive to more thoughtful living. Kindness helps us better connect not only with our close dear ones but many more people we come across during the day. I find the practice of kind attention as a helpful first step to cultivating kindness. Let's talk about that next.

20. Kind Attention

I Hate Crowds. I Don't Like Loneliness Either.

We have a love-hate relationship with our fellow beings. Large crowds, particularly in close spaces, stimulate our amygdala. Perhaps you have witnessed irrational explosions from people riding the subway. We have this instinct because for our ancestors having a lot of people around us increased our risk of acquiring lethal infections. One of them could also hurt us with a weapon. Crowds such as ten thousand people on the road trying to exit from a performance also create a feeling of competition for resources.

Our amygdala also fires when we feel lonely. Most gregarious animals when they are alone are at higher risk of becoming a prey. This applies to wildebeest as much as it does to lions. Perceived loneliness thus creates a sense of unease that we try to escape by changing our situation.

Given that we can't always force the narrow zone of social comfort we seek (not too lonely not too crowded), our amygdala senses alarm all-day long. Another instinct that signals alarm is looking at another human, particularly a stranger.

You Look Different and Scary

Researchers shockingly have found that **within about 30 milliseconds of seeing a face we conclude if the other person is trustworthy, aggressive, competent, attractive, and likable.** Many of these conclusions are wrong. Another enlightening finding is that **the more we find the other person different from us, the stronger is our amygdala activity on seeing their face.** If we see a person from a group that we associate with crime, we experience massive amygdala activation. We understandably hesitate to get into an elevator at two AM with someone we can't trust.

The instinct of amygdala reacting to a stranger was adaptive and helpful to the stone-age man who met very few people, and every encounter was a threat. Two people from different tribes walking away without punching each other's nose was an excellent meeting. But now in a big city, you could cross several thousand people from many diverse backgrounds. Such a sensory exposure is bound to give our amygdala a jog particularly if we are born with an overactive amygdala, and an underactive hippocampus and prefrontal cortex. One strategy to escape this instinct is the silent "I wish you well."

I Wish You Well (The Kind Attention Practice)

I don't know you personally, but there are two facts I know about you—you are special, and you have struggles. These two facts apply to everybody you have met and will meet in life. **Every person is priceless for a few, and every person struggles with self-worth, unresolved concerns, and unrealized desires.** With this awareness, you have a choice in how you look at others—neutrally (without paying much attention), judgmentally (looking for imperfections, or seeing others as a threat), or with kind attention. Kind attention entails sending a silent good wish to the other person—'I wish you well.' So here is the core practice #3:

> **Core practice #3: Choose to send a silent good wish to as many people as you can during the day.**

Notice that this wish is silent. You do not go around saying "I wish you well" all-day long. It might look cultish if you did that. Also, you don't have to start this practice in downtown Chicago at 2 AM in the morning. Start where you feel comfortable and feel safe.

Every time you silently wish the other person well, you wish two people well—one is the other person, and the second person is yourself. Kind attention converts looking at another person into an uplifting experience. You pull positive energy out of thin air. An excellent strategy is to **take out five minutes during the day and plan a wishing well walk.** During this time, remind yourself to let go of all planning and problem solving, and instead keep one task—silently wishing others well. You will come back uplifted from this walk.

The more you can use your eyes as a healing instrument, the higher will be the uplift to your day. This practice can change your every lived experience—meetings and conferences go easier, client encounters improve, parties become more positive, drives become less aggravating.

The practice of kindness is so powerful and such an excellent way to switch your presence from amygdala to hippocampus/PFC mode, that I have spent countless hours practicing and thinking about creative ways to bring it to our lives. Let's talk about that next.

21. Creative with Kindness

Your Presence

I am sure you know a few people you'll love to run into at the farmer's market. And you also know a few you would prefer to avoid at all cost. You like the *presence* of some people, and you are annoyed by the *presence* of some others.

Many factors feed into our presence: personality, appearance, the tone of voice, intentions, and more. Broadly, I look at presence as three distinct types: *seeking, averting, and healing*.

A person embodying seeking presence is hungry for something that will make them feel complete. It could be food, sleep, a mate, information, or something else. **We spend almost half our day in the seeking presence.**

When embodying the averting presence, we try to be safe, and avoid company or situations that take away our energy and calm. You could be running away from people, noise, pollution, buildings, places, and more.

Most days we switch from seeking to averting presence, and seldom embody a healing presence, in which we neither seek or avert anything, but become an agent of hope and healing for others (and in turn ourselves). An example of a healing presence is when trying to help someone close to you. A friend going through a breakup will need your healing presence. So will a loved one who has thrown his or her back, or a trusted colleague who just lost his or her job.

However, **waiting for visible evidence of a struggle in someone before you embody a healing presence might be a very long wait. It will bypass the enormous invisible suffering that is as universally present today as air and water on our planet.** Being creative with kindness is acknowledging the universal invisible suffering and doing your bit to help it by embodying a healing presence, remembering that **the best way to heal yourself is to try and heal someone else.**

Some Ideas

Here are a few approaches I have used to be creative about kindness by embodying a healing presence.

Over the phone—When I pick up the phone and say hello, I try to send kind attention to the person on the other side. **The first second or two of most phone calls are pure with minimal judgments. Use that time to send kind attention.** I have found this starts my phone call on a positive note, and have experienced others often perceiving the positive energy.

Hospital bed—Once I was lying in a hospital bed in the ER waiting for the test results to come back. I thought about all the patients who may have used the same bed before me and everyone who will use the bed after me. Many were surely worse off than I was. I sent silent good wishes to them all. Those thoughts and that practice uplifted me.

List of clients—When you look at the list of people you are going to meet during the day, you can choose to send them a silent good wish, wherever they are.

The doorknob—Many people touch the doorknob every day. When you use the doorknob, you can feel connected to them all, sending them a silent good wish.

Ladies who came for your mother's baby shower before you were born— Some people struggle with finding more than a few people toward whom they could be grateful. Extending your imagination, you can think of all those who have been kind to you or your family, such as all the ladies who came for your mother's baby shower before you were born.

Your mailman, delivery truck driver—They bring us all the Christmas gifts, the college acceptance letters, the checks, and of course, the bills. Think of all the humans who worked together to bring your mail to your inbox and send them your kind attention.

People who have helped you, but you don't know them—Think of the parents and teachers of your doctors and nurses who taught them the skills to help you; the family of your daycare provider; your kid's teachers' spouses; and more. Likely, you haven't met most of them, but they have touched your life through their loved ones and deserve your gratitude and kindness.

In the flight—When flying over a city, you can think of all the people in the city below, struggling with their many issues, and send them your kindness.

If you allow your imagination to fly, you can find myriad ways to be kind and countless people who you can send your silent good wish. An important place to do this is at one of the most likely places of stress—your work.

Kindness at Work

Increasingly, for many of us, work provides our core identity. We are exquisitely sensitive to our image at work. Every worker brings work to his or her home—some bring emails and paper files, and everyone brings wandering thoughts.

Almost every worker today struggles with demand-resource imbalance—trying to pack 20 pounds of sand in a ten-pound sandbag. The related stress bleeds into personal life, worsening relationships, increasing risk of separation and divorce, even lowering kid's grades. Further, workers' engagement, professionalism, creativity, safety, and client satisfaction, all take a hit when workers feel judged. **The business case for kindness at work is strong.**

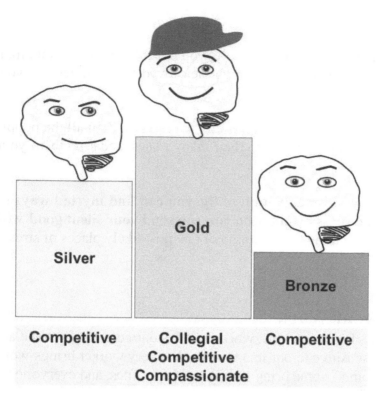

Silver — Competitive

Gold — Collegial Competitive Compassionate

Bronze — Competitive

Collegiality and compassion within a team are essential to its phenomenal success

Here are a few ideas to enhance kindness at work:

Be predictable—Workers with unpredictable colleagues and supervisors waste considerable mental energy guessing their moods and preferences, and preempting and skirting their next tantrum. That isn't a good use of time and resources. **Your predictability is a gift to keep your colleagues' amygdala calm.**

Be flexible—The higher your ability to accommodate others' preferences the more positive your work environment. Creating unnecessary and rigid rules suffocates people's mind. Rigid hierarchy and robust protocols are helpful in crises such as in war zones. In times of peace and prosperity, relative flexibility, particularly about preferences fosters engagement and creativity.

Cultivate a sense of equality—**Feeling superior or inferior, both increase discomfort and vulnerability.** When you feel superior, you work hard to maintain that hierarchy. When you feel inferior, you struggle with self-worth and meaning. Such a feeling decreases risk-taking. Hence, the **best approach is to consider everyone equal—equally worthy.**

Distribute control—With most of us overloaded at work, decreasing the load is difficult. It generally amounts to shifting the burden to someone else. **One way to reduce the perceived load is to provide control.** We feel our effort as more effortful when we perceive we have little control. To the extent feasible, allow others to carve their path to achieve the target. Further, take their input in setting the goals. Goals developed together will have greater buy-in and are more likely to be met.

Meaning—In today's economy with low unemployment rates, workers aren't just looking for a paycheck and perks. **Meaning is essential.** The younger generation even more strongly cares about work that is prosocial and helps the disadvantaged. **Aligning the daily activities with the company's overall mission and aligning the company's mission with the good of the world, is a recipe for long-term success.**

Who is happier at work?

Personal—The work environment isn't very different from a neighborhood or family. The higher the personal touch—remembering special occasions, names of your colleagues' loved ones, honoring individual culture—the kinder and more effective the workplace.

These are just a few starter ideas in the overall theme of being creative with kindness. **When you are kind toward others, you become kinder toward self.** Self-kindness, in turn, enhances kindness toward others. Self-kindness puts you in a nice upward spiral, that can nurture every aspect of our life.

22. Self-Kindness

I was once taking care of a phenomenal singer who was going through a rough patch. He had lost his voice and developed multiple medical issues. All his medical conditions were sorted out, but he wasn't bouncing back.

"I have lost my confidence. I feel judged by everyone," he said. He began looking at himself with the eyes of his recent failures, not the enormous talent and hard work he had put in all these years. I asked him who in the world completely trusts his intentions and adores him for who he is.

"My grandma," he said.
"Then sing for your grandma," I suggested.
"But she is no more," he replied.
"Well then, assume in your audience is present your grandma's spirit. Her spirit feels joyous to hear your song."

He did just that, and very soon he was back in the game.

Who Lives in Your Head?
Be very careful about who you allow to live in your head. People who live in your brain change your brain.

If you do not carefully tend to the garden of your brain, then people who judge you, demean you, don't trust your capabilities, will spread the weeds of self-doubt, self-judgment, and low self-worth. Who do you think about when you are driving back from work or at the end of a party? On many days we think about the grumpy ones. And if anyone played nasty, they are bound to take a vast real estate. With this default instinct, negative feedbacks and judgments dominate our thoughts, just like an extra spoon of chili powder can spoil an otherwise perfect bowl of soup.

**The grumpy and nasty people
occupy a disproportionate
real estate in our head**

While completely ignoring negative feedbacks isn't possible or desirable, it will be good to keep that feedback in a more holistic perspective. Here is what I try to do to practice self-kindness:

- I isolate disapprovals. (If you don't like my handwriting, that doesn't mean you dislike my accent.)
- I consider someone upset as hurt, and do not take their negative emotions personally
- **I consider present failure as reflective of past effort and not necessarily how things will work out in the future**
- I strive to surprise those who don't believe in me
- I believe the right about me is much more than the wrong
- **I interpret critique as a pointer that others think I am capable of better**

- I try my best to apply all of the above not just to me, but to all others

Take negative feedback in stride; Believe in yourself

Each of above perspective positively biases me and helps me overcome my inherent negativity bias. An intentional positive perspective truly helps—it helps me take critique in stride, savor the praise, and keep the good energy through the day.

The bottom line: *Look at yourself with the eyes of the person who loves/trusts/values you unconditionally and believe in those who believe in you.*

How Do You Define Success?

Imagine you are the family elder surrounded by three generations of your descendants who have gathered around you to listen to the family stories

143

at Thanksgiving dinner. Which stories will you be most proud to share? The ones that talk about how you worked hard and kept good intentions despite your failures, or the ones where you made millions by duping the innocent? Perhaps there are a few in this world who will revel in the second group of stories. But for most of us, it is the first kind of stories that will be told and retold as part of the family legacy.

The world, unfortunately, is now replete with examples of people who cared just about the outcomes. The short-term quarter to quarter earnings reports with fortunes made and lost in the blink of an eye promote success-at-any-cost attitude.

For each success, we experience several failures. And **the sorrow of defeat feels much deeper than the joy of victory.** How long did you enjoy the last promotion? How long would you be upset if you are passed over for promotion? Most people say a few days at the most in response to the first question, and perhaps a lifetime in response to the second.

Such a disposition makes us vulnerable. It also creates an unstable anchorless state of the mind that is highly dependent on the outcomes for feeling good.

A much better approach is to focus on effort and intentions. Your effort and even more, your intentions, are in your control. **Feel worthy if you gave your best and had the best intentions.** Outcomes aren't in your control. Results depend on many more variables than you can influence. Here is my Forbes quote of the day from a few years ago.

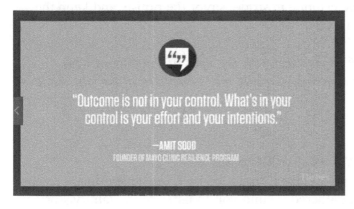

Focusing excessively on the outcome is a sure way to hurt the effort. A gymnast who constantly thinks about the gold medal during her performance will slip. Her mind is too much into the future to focus on the present. While the gymnast who tries to give her personal best, will delight the audience and judges, and is more likely to land the gold.

The bottom line: *Anchor your self-worth on effort and intentions and not the outcomes. Judge others for their effort and intentions and not the outcomes.*

What is Your Worth?

We are living two lives—material and spiritual. Wealth in these two domains has different parameters. The material life values us by our salary, bank account, job profile, and more. The spiritual life assesses us by the principles we embody, by the purpose we are serving. **Material gains that entail spiritual loss are almost always a net loss. Spiritual gains that involve material loss are often a net gain. The best pursuits help you grow spiritually and materially.**

You have a choice where you anchor your self-worth. I believe you will be massively undervaluing yourself if you root your self-worth in your paycheck. **In this infinitely vast universe made of trillions of galaxies, no matter how wealthy you are, your material net worth is infinitely small.**

However, we all have access to the most precious of the principles—compassion and forgiveness—that are time transcending. Many of us also have access to our faith, that again is infinitely precious. **Anchoring your self-worth in your principles and your faith makes you priceless.**

The dollar value the world gives to you is a moving target. Our possessions are also very transient; billions can evaporate in the blink of an eye. An excessive focus on our material possessions and valuing ourselves based on what we have cannot accord lasting peace and contentment. Further, in the language of the contemplatives, the mind is subtler than matter. The subtle can never be satisfied with the gross. Hence the mind needs the spiritual feast to feel content.

The bottom line: *Value yourself not by material net worth, but by the principles you embody, the people and purpose you serve, and your faith.*

23. Drop One

Most tobacco users try their best to quit smoking. But nicotine is a tough addiction. It is as if after a period of use, the brain starts needing nicotine to function normally. Another reason quitting smoking is so difficult is because trying to quit tobacco often leads to weight gain. When investigators tried to prevent weight gain during a quit attempt, participants failed at both—they couldn't quit and also gained weight. It was almost like we have a central source of vitality or will power. If you tap on this resource too much, the system fails.

It is for this reason, whenever planning a behavioral change, I suggest working on personal stressors and optimizing the state of mind (developing stress resilience) as a first step. **A cooperative and happy mind finds it easier to embrace dietary changes, physical activity, and more.**

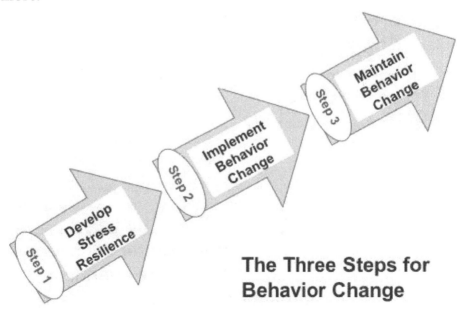

The Three Steps for Behavior Change

We are at that stage of progress in SMART where we can expand beyond the resilience practices to pick one or two additional ideas. Here I suggest you examine your life and drop one unhealthy habit. As an illustration, I have selected three of them: prolonged sitting, habitual multitasking, and a daily dose of excessive news.

Prolonged Sitting

In the knowledge economy, our work demands that we focus on a screen for hours on end and type using both our hands. This requirement is best met in the sitting position in a safe place, so that we can free our attention from the need to maintain balance and secure safety. We have thus become chairman or chairwoman. **The sedentary lifestyle of an overworked person results in a relaxed body and an active mind, while we strive for an active body and a relaxed mind.**

The physical cost of our inactivity is high. **Very quickly after sitting, our cholesterol, triglyceride and blood sugar levels rise, our muscles start atrophying, and bones get weaker.** The result is about a 25 percent

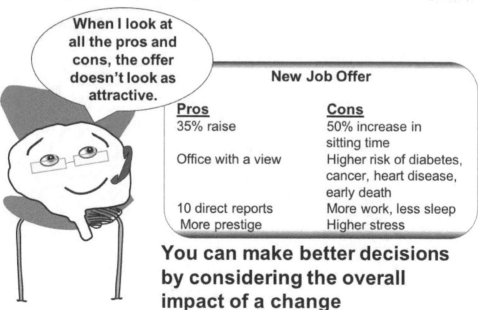

increase in mortality, a 15 percent increase in cancer prevalence, a 20 percent increase in death from heart disease and cancer, and a 90 percent increased risk of diabetes with prolonged sitting. **In one report, an hour of extra sitting watching TV decreased life span by 22 minutes.**

How to fix this? In simple words, **instead of being a chairperson, be a messenger boy.** Whenever you can, let your legs bear the weight and not your chair. Exercising three to five times a week alone won't do it. Remaining agile throughout the day is equally important.

Start with organizing your space to maximize walking. Stand up every so often, march in place, stretch your arms, wander in your office—whatever gets you active. Stand and walk while taking phone calls, watching TV commercials, and at the end of the match or board game. Some experts suggest splitting a half hour time into three units using the formula 20-8-2. Spend 20 minutes sitting, eight minutes standing and two minutes walking. I tried it but found it too cumbersome. I find the following two suggestions practical:

- **Stand up about once an hour and take a short walk every two hours**
- **Spend at least part of your day as messenger boy (walk over for meetings, schedule walking meetings, stand while talking on the phone)**

Standing from sitting position is one activity where the rewards are immediate. Within 60 to 90 seconds of standing, your metabolism kicks up. Calorie burn rate goes up by 30 to 50 percent. It's good for your heart, your lungs, and your brain. **In the long term, by being agile through the day, you are being kind to yourself.**

Habitual Multitasking

I am going through the airport security check with two kids, seven pieces of luggage, and impatient staff and fellow passengers. If you chastise me for multitasking in that situation, my response will be, "You got to be kidding." I cannot do one thing at a time at that moment and annoy my fellow passengers.

But if I multitask while reading a book to my child (and get caught trying to skip pages) or listening to my spouse about her difficult meeting, then I

149

am shortchanging others and myself. So, **thoughtful multitasking isn't bad, while multitasking that becomes a habit is counterproductive.**

The problem is we are a creature of habit and momentum. Multitasking that might have started as necessity becomes a habit. A quick review of one aspect of the neuroscience of learning might help here.

When you ski for the first time, your entire brain lights up. You can't plan a party while doing downhill ski. But after practicing for ten years, the brain no longer needs to commit all its resources to ski.

In a novice skier, the entire brain lights up

An experienced skier needs to commit little brain area

With experience, you use lesser brain real estate to accomplish the same task

The brain relegates this activity to the much smaller subconscious subcortical area, the same it does for brushing your teeth, taking a shower, or using your fork.

Once that switch happens, the areas that host conscious activity are freed up. They aren't, however, entirely freed up. For example, if you listen to the traffic report while driving, you won't see a gorilla or an elephant standing roadside. Our brain by design is a serial mono-tasker that can train itself into multi-tasking but doesn't quite totally master the multi-tasking skills.

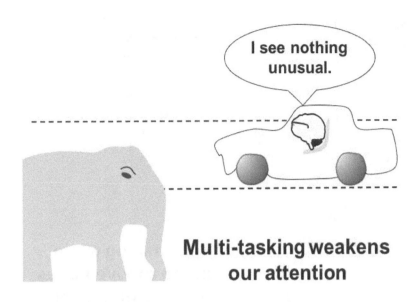

Multi-tasking weakens our attention

So, given that we are compelled to multitask in some situations and our brain learns with repetition of an activity, it'll help to come up with the right multitasking balance. Here are four ideas:

1. **Avoid multitasking in a high-risk activity such as driving**: However mundane the driving experience and familiar the roads, a surprise can happen at any moment. Such a surprise, not attended well, can seed a regret of a lifetime.

2. **Avoid multitasking in relationships**: Avoid looking at a computer screen or sorting your mail when talking to your spouse or while listening to your teenager how her day went. Avoid skipping pages when reading a book to a kindergartener! Also, avoid checking emails in a meeting merely out of curiosity.

My wife always catches me when I multi-task while talking to her. Her comment – "You sound much more agreeable!"

Multi-tasking while talking to loved ones hurts the quality of relationships

3. **Avoid multitasking as a habit**: Try not to multitask just because you can. The more your effort to discover novelty in a mundane activity, the better your learning, performance, and joy.

4. **Choose intentional monotasking once in a while**: Try to do something simple like loading dishwasher, vacuuming, eating, or watching kids play tennis—with full attention. It will sprinkle fresh joy in what may otherwise not be an engaging experience, at the same time training your attention muscles.

Daily Dose of Excessive News

If you are like me, you want the news channels filled with positive and uplifting news. And if you are like me, you spend more time watching and reading negative and not positive news. **Research shows that even when we prefer and like the positive, our eyeballs spend more time tracking and locking on to the negative.**

The news channels know this, and that's why they tickle your amygdala every day. They take the local news through this negativity filter, cull out the most sensational negative items, and thus create the national press. That's why the national news has a much more negative flavor compared to the local news.

However, **much of what we watch in the national news is not actionable. It only increases our heart rate and blood pressure, and the risk of stress and post-traumatic stress disorder.** It is also a colossal waste of time.

An accomplished physician colleague once shared with me about his frustration at inability to find time with the family. We sat down and took a close look at his daily activities. He shockingly realized that he was spending two hours every day watching the news. He cut it down to 15-minutes, much to the delight of his family, and his blood pressure.

I suggest you carefully log the amount of time you spend with the news channels. If it is more than 15 minutes, you are wasting your time while increasing your risk of a variety of medical conditions and shortening your life. Decrease that time to 15 minutes or less and replace it with another nurturing activity that both entertains you and gives your brain some restful moments.

24. Restful Moments

Our brain processes a large number of inputs all-day long. It thus produces more waste products than it can metabolize or excrete, very much like the downtown district in a large city that is too active during the day to accomplish all its cleaning operations. The district cleans itself at night. So does the brain—through sleep.

Sleep is the time when the garbage trucks of the brain take away all the dead neurotransmitters and other chemicals through the channels called glymphatic channels. These channels remain shut during the day. Until recently clearing the brain only at night worked for us. However, of late we have run into two problems. One, almost every innovation in technology has caused brain overload, creating too much gunk that can't wait for the night. Two, restful, restorative sleep has become increasingly elusive for many of us.

An overloaded sleep-deprived brain is a problem. **Constant brain activity without adequate rest is a recipe for a decline in the quality of our experience, predisposes to illness, and eventually degrades the structural integrity of our brain.** Almost every entity in nature that has survived for a long time has developed a mechanism to rest and rejuvenate. Let's learn from the wisdom of the corn fields.

The Fields are Resting

I live in corn country. I derive great inspiration and wisdom from the corn fields. It is fantastic to see the collaboration between sunlight, the fields, the wind, all facilitated by thousands of farmers who act as a catalyst in making all this happen. Each spring I witness the well-planned tillage and then seeding. Within a few weeks emerge a hint of saplings that grow fast, sometimes an inch a day. The plant exceeds my height in a month and before you know it, begins sporting tassels and ears with silk. Ears mature, are harvested, and one day while driving by the fields, I find the fields leveled again. What follows is Minnesota winter in which the fields hibernate beneath a pile of snow, for months. At this time, one might say that nothing is happening, but this is a crucial phase in the fields' yearly cycle. The fields are resting.

If the fields don't rest, then they will be tired next spring, and none of this cycle will repeat. Like a child who wakes up tired and groggy if she had blocked nose and kept coughing all night, the fields that do not adequately rest (over-farmed), get depleted. **Rest isn't a waste of time. It is essential for you to value rest.**

Many different practices can rest your brain. The gratitude practices discussed previously, the two-minute rule, and curious moments all will relax you. Play of almost any kind, running, stroll, family meal, nap, music, calming movie, art, coloring, writing, reading, gardening, horseback riding, bicycling, intimate time—all are relaxing.

In general, if you spent the day in chaos, your brain will need quiet time by yourself. On the other hand, if you spent the day in a quiet office just by yourself, you might need social time. Align your rest with your brain's current hunger.

While our whole body needs rest, our brain, heart, and eyes are the three organs that need the most rest. One of the best rests for your eyes is to close them gently, for the heart is to take deep breaths that slow your heart and smoothen its beats, and for the brain is to give it freedom from

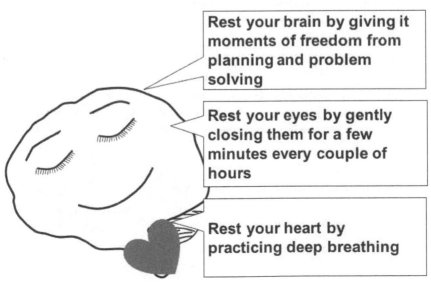

Rest your brain by giving it moments of freedom from planning and problem solving

Rest your eyes by gently closing them for a few minutes every couple of hours

Rest your heart by practicing deep breathing

planning and problem solving and feed it uplifting emotions. A good meditation program combines all three.

A Few Basics

I find a lot of parallels between swimming and meditating. Both practices have been around for thousands of years, both involve considerable training and attention, both need deliberate effort and while to some extent are natural to us, need intentional practice to master. There are two key differences though. One, meditation isn't practiced as a competitive sport. Two, meditation is considered by many as a spiritual practice.

A common mistake is that we expect meditation to act much faster than it can. In swimming equivalent, we expect us to swim like dolphins in a few weeks. Realistically, when you start swimming, you first learn to not be a brick. You put your face in the water, hold your breath for a few seconds, and learn to trust your instructor. Then you learn to be a tadpole—floating and performing basic strokes. It takes several years to advance to the stage of dolphins where watching you swim effortlessly and playfully becomes delightful to a lot of people.

Similarly, in meditation, the first step is to develop three core abilities:
- The ability to sit still for a few minutes
- The ability to practice deep breathing
- The ability to focus your mind

I suggest you start with a simple 10-minute practice that gives your heart, brain, and eyes a good relaxation. One such practice is 'Calm and Energize,' a relaxing micro-workout of these three body parts. I practice it most days, sometime during the middle of the day to recharge myself, and it has never failed in calming and energizing me.

The practice involves the following steps:
- Notice a flower as it opens, attending to its details.
- After the flower has opened, gently close your eyes. Let your eyelids touch each other as gently as the petals touch each other.

- Bring attention to your breath and observe its flow without changing it.
- Feel the flow of your breath at the tip of your nostrils.
- Start deep slow breathing synchronizing it with the flute sounds.
- Observe the breath flowing from your nose to the heart, calming and energizing your heart. Continue this practice for about 90 seconds.
- Observe the breath flowing from your heart to your eyes, calming and energizing your eyes. Continue this practice for about 90 seconds.
- Observe the breath flowing from your heart to your brain, calming and energizing your brain. Continue this practice for about 90 seconds.
- Send silent gratitude to one person in your life who truly cares about you.
- Give your entire body a nice stretch.
- Set a positive intention for the rest of the day.
- Open your eyes.

Here is the link to this practice on YouTube: https://www.youtube.com/watch?v=IGDJjO6WEb8

If you wish to access additional meditations, you can find them at myhappinesspal.com.

Several excellent authors and teachers have written and developed videos and apps on meditation. You are welcome to explore a few of them and find the one that works best for you. If you prefer a faith-based practice, prayer is equally powerful.

I suggest you invest at least ten minutes in the middle of a busy day resting your brain. Practice deep breathing in the background in that time and let go of planning and problem-solving. Deep breathing will give your brain an opportunity to clear itself of the accumulated toxic neurotransmitters and other chemicals, so it remains fresh and energy replete most of the day.

25. Summary

The core practices from the first three modules of the SMART program are noted below.

> **Core practice #1: First thing in the morning, think about five people in your life who mean a lot to you and send them your silent gratitude.**

> **Core practice #2: Give two minutes of undivided attention to at least one person each day who deserves that attention but isn't presently getting it.**

> **Core practice #3: Choose to send a silent good wish to as many people as you can during the day.**

Integrate these practices in your life before adding another practice from module IV. Also, at this stage consider adding a sitting meditation practice, along with dropping at least one unhealthy habit (prolonged sitting, habitual multitasking, or a daily dose of excessive news).

Here are the four key learning points I wish to recap before moving to module 4:

1. Kindness isn't a choice
2. Kindness has many flavors
3. Drop one unhealthy habit
4. Develop a personal practice to clear your brain

Kindness Isn't a Choice

While our body feasts on oxygen, calories, and other nutrients, our mind needs a daily dose of uplifting emotions. You can get uplifting emotions from watching a funny video, completing a successful project, getting a raise, and more. But more powerful and sustainable than all of these is receiving kindness from and giving kindness to loved ones, friends, colleagues, and others. **When kindness is missing, anger, hatred, and envy fill the place that hurt the person giving as well as receiving these negative emotions.** We have enough of that already on our planet.

Further, raising a child is a collaborative effort of tens of thousands of people in a city. We arrive in the world utterly helpless and dependent on the kindness of others to make it to the first birthday and beyond. Our vulnerable young ones won't survive without kindness. Kindness thus isn't a frivolous pleasing option. It is an absolute necessity if we are to survive and thrive on this planet.

Fill your brain with kindness, so it has no space left for anger, envy, or hatred

Kindness has Many Flavors

Kindness expresses itself in countless ways. You can show kindness to fellow humans—loved ones, friends, colleagues, neighbors, strangers, to the self, to the pets and other animals, even to the stuff you own. How we treat a rental car can tell a lot about us. **Those who treat a rental car with the same care as they treat their own car are the salt of the earth.**

You can express your kindness in words, in actions, or both. Some of us are good with words, others with actions, and still others with both. A few, unfortunately, have the right intentions but don't have the energy or the skills to translate those actions into words and actions. It is good to keep this in mind when you come across someone ungrateful or unkind. **Research shows that a fair proportion of the predisposition to lack of kindness is genetic.**

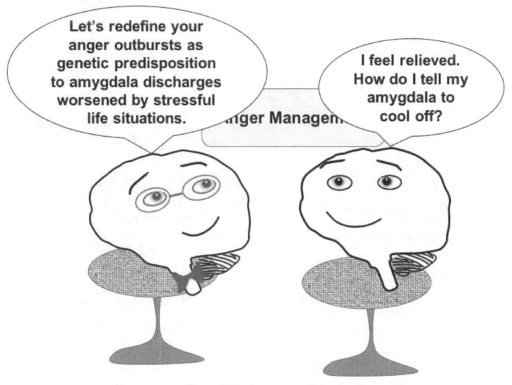

**Connecting biology with behavior
can be empowering and validating**

This realization isn't meant to make you vulnerable. It is to recognize the underlying biology, which can help you remain compassionate toward others and self, and thus in balance.

We discussed several creative ideas to bring kindness to your personal and professional life. **Kindness is like salt, that enhances the taste of**

most dishes in which it is mixed. Like salt, sometimes kindness can be excessive. You don't want to be kind to a rabid dog, or a person who embodies such behavior. Your kindness toward them will be construed as weakness, make you vulnerable, and won't reflect your kindness toward self. A lack of kindness toward others in such situations is sometimes justified if it helps you be kind toward yourself.

Drop One Unhealthy Habit

We make habits, and then our habits make us. Forming and dropping a habit takes time and a good amount of mental energy. Our goal in the first three parts of SMART has been to decrease the energy drain by decreasing mind wandering and infusing positive energy by focusing on gratitude, novelty, and kindness.

Once your mind is clearer, your stress is lower, and you have greater will power and attention bandwidth, it will be easier for you to work on other aspects of life. Here I suggest picking at least one of the three unhealthy habits that affect almost everyone I meet today. They are prolonged sitting, habitual multitasking, and daily excessive news.

Pick the one that you struggle with the most and find most amenable to change.

Develop a Personal Practice to Clear Your Brain

When scientists researched the benefits of exercise on our heart health, they laid the groundwork for gyms, healthy living centers, wellness coaches, and nutrition. No one calls a person running at 5:30 AM in the morning in the neighborhood as crazy. I know several people who leave their home at 4 AM and run for about an hour each day. They do this most of the year, even when it is ten below zero outside. We admire them at parties and want to know their secret.

As we are researching brain science in the current generation, there is an excellent chance that in the next few decades, a personal practice to clear your brain of its waste products, will be considered as routine as healthy eating or jogging for the heart.

Presently, we need to continue to innovate, so we develop simpler and highly effective programs. If meditation is expensive, challenging, and requires a significant time commitment, then it will remain confined to a select few. Making it simple, short, scalable and accessible will bring it to the masses.

It is also essential to define meditation in the right way, so we don't feel it belongs to a religion or geography. **My definition of meditation is *Intentional, grateful and compassionate attention.***

Let's turn now to the fourth and final module of the SMART program, Resilient Mindset.

MODULE IV
Resilient Mindset

The fourth step, resilient mindset, helps you cultivate a mind that thinks thoughts and interprets the world guided by timeless values, ones that put you in the upward spiral of life.

26. The Committee

I don't know about you, most days I have a committee meeting inside my head. This committee has many members; they often crosstalk and interrupt each other. It's a bit like a soap opera. I recognize three of them for sure. Allow me to introduce you to them.

The Three Members

The three members are *Mr. Greedy, Mr. Fearful, and Mr. Rational*. It might be best to meet them imagining my hungry brain looking at a donut.

Mr. Greedy (Love the donut)—On a day I am hungry, my reward center (Mr. Greedy) imagines the donut to be part of my body since the calorie load will come in handy fighting the next Neanderthal which can happen any moment.

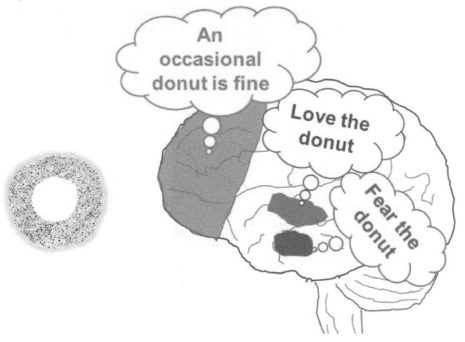

Your different brain areas evaluating a donut

Mr. Fearful (Fear the donut)—Mr. Fearful is worried that if I don't eat the donut, someone else will. A different fear in the modern world is the fear of calories—of what the cholesterol needles in the donut can do to my body.

Mr. Rational (An occasional donut is okay)—Mr. Rational focuses on the long term and prioritizes values and meaning. This part of my brain is attracted to the donut but also recognizes that I could do without all the extra calories.

Do you see how these three members give me three different inputs? Somewhere in the brain, and nobody knows the precise location, these three inputs integrate, and a single decision is made. The decision, however, isn't easy. If you decide to pass, you might feel a little frustrated (technically called reward depletion). If you choose to eat, you will likely feel guilty. (This example won't apply to you if you don't like donuts. Replace donuts with another relished calorie-dense food item.)

Do you see how **our brain by design is a conflicted organ**?

The Conflicted Brain

Different members of our brain are in a constant tug of war, trying to get their agenda honored. Of all the organs in the body, our brain is unique in its conflicts. Your kidneys aren't conflicted right now. They know what to do. Your right and left lungs do not compete. Your right lung isn't inhaling while the left lung is exhaling.

In daily life, we face countless conflicts. Should I take care of me or others, focus on money or meaning, short term or long term. A single email offers so many options—read, delete, save, respond, flag, post to social media, and more. **If you get a hundred emails in a day, that's six hundred decision points, just with emails.**

Further, because of our brain's conflicted design and the need to balance multiple agendas, I cannot trust my brain to think, speak or be rational all the time, particularly when my brain is tired.

If you have said or done something irrational, or sometimes have crazy thoughts that aren't becoming of who you are, then recognize that this predisposition is part of the brain's design. This awareness has helped me in two ways. One, I have become kinder to others—loved ones, friends, colleagues, strangers—who have momentary benign lapses of rationality. Two, I have realized that I am sometimes blind to my blind spots. The awareness of my brain's limitations not only keeps me humble but also has sparked a search for the principles that I can trust.

That search has been very rewarding and has led me to the five principles of resilience thinking that I next share with you.

27. Resilience Thinking

Resilience thinking is choosing thoughts that will help you become stronger, kinder, and happier. It has hope, inspiration, and courage in it. It is sensible and truthful. **Resilience thinking honors the preferences and needs of the individual at the same time supporting the collective.**

While there are days we are rational and predictable, on days you have thrown your back, got a D grade, have a hormonal imbalance, or couldn't sleep past 3 AM, rationality may be inaccessible to your mind. These are the days when we need a GPS for our mind.

The GPS

When I first started driving in the pre-GPS era, I would stick to the right lane. Before I knew, it would become an exit lane. Unable to change the lanes in time, I would end up taking the exit, and invariably end in the cul-de-sac of an unknown neighborhood. My wife and I would add 30-minutes of 'getting-lost time' to our calendar for each commute.

Now with GPS in our phones and on the dashboard, I am no longer afraid of getting lost. The same holds for the mind. **If your mind has a set of guiding principles to align its journey through the day and knows how to quickly recover if it takes an undesired exit, then the drive, even on unfamiliar roads will become relaxed.**

The mind needs a reliable GPS because, without that guidance, the mind invariably veers off the road and doesn't know how to recover in time. Five principles contribute to the design of the mind's GPS—Gratitude, Compassion, Acceptance, Meaning, and Forgiveness.

> **Core practice #4: Align your day with one or more of the five principles—gratitude, compassion, acceptance, meaning, and forgiveness.**

Since five is too many to remember at any moment, we have assigned them a day. Mondays are our days of gratitude, Tuesdays of compassion, and so on per the schematic below. Saturdays are our days of celebration and Sundays of reflection/prayer.

Monday	Gratitude
Tuesday	Compassion
Wednesday	Acceptance
Thursday	Meaning
Friday	Forgiveness
Saturday	Celebration
Sunday	Reflection/Prayer

These five principles stood out in my original search for finding constructs that are timeless, research-validated, and consistently engage the pre-frontal cortex.

The idea of having a theme for the day isn't meant to create a nerdy rigid structure. You don't say that you can't be compassionate on Thursdays since Tuesday is the assigned day for compassion! The idea is to be flexible and flowing. With time, the five principles will merge into a single daily practice. Until then, at least for the initial few weeks, try to experience your day keeping the flavor of the principle assigned to the day. Here are five ways you can do it.

Read, Think, Write, Share, Practice

The easiest way to bring a principle to your life is to read about it. Spend a few minutes reading about the principle—from this book, another book, or a website.

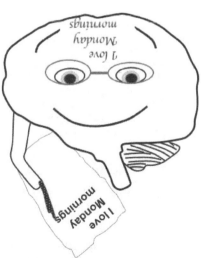

You make an idea your own by thinking and meditating on it. You connect the learning with what you already know and understand what it means to you. Ask yourself—What does it mean to lower my gratitude threshold? How do I expand my zone of compassion? Why is acceptance so tricky? How can I connect my meaning with everyday activities? What is the relationship between forgiveness and physical health?

Writing on a paper writes in your brain

With deep thinking, you'll begin to develop your unique insights most

169

pertinent to your life. Since the nature of the mind is to forget, writing your thoughts will help you remember them, integrate them in your life, and recap them next time you need the same insight. **When you write something externally, you simultaneously write that file in your brain.**

One of the best ways to integrate a concept is to share with someone. A word of caution here. It is best not to be preachy. While you may be excited about an idea, others may not be on the same page or may have different priorities.

Best to give others space

So, first, create a like-minded circle of people who are interested in discussing the deeper aspects of life. When you start building such a circle, you might notice that most such people will have faced considerable adversity in their life or witnessed it in others.

The fifth and final approach is to practice the principles. I have shared formal practices around gratitude and compassion (kindness) in the previous few sections and will share more ideas in the following pages. One way I bring acceptance into my life is to think about how these six words can help me—I am enough. I have enough. Similarly, plan pre-emptive forgiveness when you are going to meet someone at a party who has an unparalleled ability to annoy you.

Each of the approaches helps you be proactive about the principle. **The proactive approach builds resilience muscles in your mind (much more than the reactive approach).** The key ingredient to the proactive approach, that applies to all the five principles that follow is *lowering the threshold*.

Lowering the Threshold

The statisticians will tell you that most entities in the world follow one of the two distributions—categorical or continuous. Categorical distributions are Yes/No. For example, you ate breakfast this morning or not, or you were born before or after 1970.

Continuous distributions have infinite possibilities. Some of the entities that follow such distribution are your blood pressure, body weight (and BMI), blood sugar, skin color or more. For such distributions, we often set certain criteria. We might say people are considered to have hypertension or diabetes beyond a threshold number of blood pressure or blood sugar. The same applies to the practice of the principles. No one is perfectly ungrateful or compassionate. People vary in their disposition depending on their genes, and early life and adult experiences.

The practice of the principles follows a continuous distribution. Hence, when I talk about becoming grateful or compassionate, I am only suggesting lowering the threshold. Thus, you can wait to be grateful to someone who rescues you from the quicksand, or you can choose to be grateful for a warm smile.

Our goal is to train ourselves so our threshold to practice the principles is lower—which will effectively change us as a person. You are no longer a visitor to the planet of kindness; you live there.

28. Gratitude (on Mondays)

If life were a pizza, gratitude is its topping. While you can eat pizza without the topping, it won't be as delicious. Similarly, while gratitude isn't essential to living, it remarkably enhances the flavor of life. **Gratitude is being blessed, knowing that you are blessed, and being thankful for it.**

Grateful is Humble

Being grateful is being humble. A moment of pure gratitude is one filled with contentment. Gratitude also gifts you the humble recognition of your blessings. You recognize that most of what you have—your physical health, your material possessions, your success, your fame—has come to you not just from hard work and good intentions, but also a bit of luck and the gift of grace.

Humility does wonders to relationships. The humble people attract others by enhancing their self-worth. I am sure you have been around enough people who believe that the sun rises just for them. I am also sure you don't want to be in the same room with these people.

For two people with equal merit, we want the humble (the likes of Neil Armstrong) to win. Similarly, **we are more likely to forgive the mistakes of the humble and well-meaning. Humility that takes away false pride and hubris allows you to accept vulnerability, thereby minimizing fear.** Humility and gratitude together also help you see the good in not so good, and the phenomenal in the ordinary, like a little girl at my daughter's elementary school.

The Happy Little Girl

This little girl, let's call her Crystal, was known to many as the happiest kid in the school. I asked her about what made her so happy. She had come from an impoverished country. She said, "I am happy because the grass is so green and soft." "What else," I asked. She said, "The swing sets work, and the sky is so blue."

We all come with the gratitude software installed, the key is to activate it with small daily happenings. Big things will only happen rarely. But little things happen all the time.

This girl had a low threshold to feel grateful, which is what made her happier. An excellent perspective to bring greater gratitude, and thus happiness in your life is to understand the different depths of gratitude.

I am happy because the grass is green and soft, the swing sets work, and the sky is so blue.

A little girl taught me that the key to life-long happiness is to notice and savor the ordinary

The Five Depths of Gratitude

Gratitude comes in five depths. At the most superficial level are people who are perennially ungrateful. Then are people who wait for something big to happen to be grateful, such as a promotion, an award or winning large sums of money. Level three are grateful for simple and ordinary—a smile, a glass of water, good night's sleep. Level four are grateful period. They are grateful to be alive and breathing; everything else is a bonus for them. Finally, at level five are people who are grateful even for adversity.

Matthew Henry, a Bible scholar in the 17th century, was once robbed in the streets of London. He wrote, "Let me be thankful, first, because he never robbed me before…" Matthew Henry practiced gratitude at level five—he could find gratitude even in adversity. **Gratitude is a perfect way to reframe your life's challenges, finding what went right within what went wrong.**

Deep Breath

Take a deep breath that fills the entirety of your lungs. If you were able to do that, recognize that countless millions can't take a deep breath because of heart or lungs disease, chest wall pain, or excessive pollution. That recognition will help you be grateful for the ordinary and the simple.

Some of the saddest words I have heard are from a gentleman who divorced his wife after two decades of marriage and then regretted. He said, "I divorced the woman I loved." With years of togetherness, he stopped appreciating the countless little ways she brought joy to his life. Instead, he started focusing on the imperfections.

Like kindness, when you fill your brain with gratitude, other negative emotions tend to stay outside

That's the problem with a lack of gratitude. **When we do not prioritize appreciation and gratefulness, the space gets filled with prejudices, regrets, hurts, anger, and more.** The latter feelings deplete energy. With the energy so depleted, you have little left to give to the world, let alone yourself. No wonder, the practice of gratitude has been shown to improve physical health, emotional wellbeing, and relationship quality in several studies.

Living it

The five ways you can bring greater gratitude in your life is through reading, thinking, writing, and sharing about gratitude, and committing to one or two gratitude practices.

Read about gratitude on the web or in the books. The words you read act as a catalyst to start your thought process. **I believe every day we should learn something uplifting to negate the downdraft that many of us receive from the world.**

Think about what gratitude means to you. Investigate your personal beliefs that may be preventing you from being grateful. Also, think about how gratitude can help you. Explore some unique ways you can bring greater gratitude in your life.

Many people I know vouch for maintaining a gratitude journal. Writing such a journal gives you a pause in your daily life, and since most of us do not experience extraordinary events every day, **writing a gratitude journal deepens your gratitude, so you find meaning in the simple and ordinary.** (I have written two journals to help your practice—*The Resilience Journal* tracks the SMART program, and *Happier Mornings Calmer Evenings*, that focuses on gratitude and kindness.)

One of the best ways to create meaningful connections is through principles. Friendships that are strengthened by the thread of selfish interests aren't authentic and won't last long. But friendships that are nurtured by the timeless principles become stronger with each exchange. Hence, **it is worthwhile to find likeminded friends with whom you can have gratitude-filled conversations without feeling awkward.**

The fifth and final way to bring gratitude is to practice it. The morning gratitude practice and the gratitude jar are two ideas. Sending grateful emails, a small gift, a text, a social media post, or delivering a message of gratitude in person—these are all great approaches to practice gratitude and lift yourself and the world around you.

A word of caution. **Be very careful with talking about gratitude to someone in a tough situation** such as caring for a sick child, in mourning, healing from a broken relationship, job loss, or another such adversity. Focus more on compassion, support, and validation. Your comments about gratitude could be annoying to them. Also, **best not to use gratitude as a way to compare yourself with others.** If someone is telling about their financial hardships, right at that time expressing gratitude for how well your stocks have done is a bad idea. Expressing gratitude for your success that happened at the cost of someone else will also sound shallow.

Honey, the drug company has sent a very nice letter. It says they are grateful for your diabetes and high cholesterol.

Expressions of gratitude that lack humility, compassion, and common sense can be counter-productive

In general, **gratitude is most useful and healing when it keeps the company of compassion.** Before we proceed to compassion, pause and think about what you are grateful for and who you feel grateful toward today. Next, I share an excerpt from my journal, *Happier Mornings Calmer Evenings*. Fill the boxes below if you feel up to it.

Today I am thankful for…

Today I feel grateful to…

A related thought I wish to leave you with is that sometimes others' minds aren't ready for gratitude when they are stuck in unmet personal needs. Addressing those needs as a first step frees them to feel grateful.

**A mind filled with
unfulfilled wants
struggles with feeling grateful**

I hope you find many reasons to be grateful today, and in the days, weeks, months, and years ahead.

29. Compassion (on Tuesdays)

If gratitude is the topping, compassion is the base of the pizza. **Compassion is so essential to us humans that I believe without compassion we won't survive as a species.** However, we often do not prioritize living a compassionate life. That is partly because we often confuse compassion for empathy.

What is Compassion?

Empathy is recognizing and feeling another person's pain. Empathy worsens mood by activating the brain areas that host negative emotions. **Compassion is recognizing and feeling another person's pain *with an active desire to help and heal*. Compassion energizes and uplifts by activating your reward network.**

A full compassionate response has four components: You recognize others' pain, you do not judge them for their pain (i.e. you validate their pain), you nurture an active desire to help, and you translate this desire into action. Compassion thus is a lot about action.

Unfortunately, many don't realize the real physiological and psychological benefits of compassion. We also don't realize that we can solve a vast majority of personal emotional pain and interpersonal problems by cultivating compassion, for self and others.

With research showing that college students are increasingly getting less compassionate, I believe the world desperately needs a compassionate spirit (much more than competitive spirit), to honor our differences, savor our similarities, and transcend the old silos that divide us into increasingly isolated factions.

Compassion is essential for the success that takes you and your team to greatness. **A competitive team that is collegial and compassionate is much more likely to achieve phenomenal success compared to a group driven by pure ambition.**

Three rules about pain, particularly emotional pain, that I mention next will help your compassion journey.

Your Brain on Pain

Our brain has committed areas that activate when we feel pain (sometimes called the pain matrix). Three distinct features of our pain matrix have helped me develop deeper compassion.

Rule #1: Your pain is my pain
Concerning the pain, our definition of self extends beyond us. **Our brain's pain network lights up on seeing someone else in pain, especially if we feel close to that person. Thus, helping others in distress is helping yourself.**

Rule #2: Emotional pain is the same as physical pain
The same brain network hosts emotional and physical pain. Some researchers believe emotional pain has hijacked the physical pain pathways. In one study, Tylenol was significantly beneficial in improving emotional distress. Thus, **people hurting from an insult are hurting as much if not more, as someone with an ankle sprain.**

Rule #3: Imaginary pain is the same as the real pain
For our brain, imagination engages the same areas as the real experience. Imagining playing piano or violin activates the same regions that activate with the real thing. The terror of nightmares is real. Fear of failure and rejection feels like failure and rejection itself.

Of course, the benefit of imagination doesn't extrapolate to every experience. Imagined exercise won't build aerobic capacity in your body!

The benefit of imaginary experience doesn't apply to every aspect of life

Here is the bottom line:

- **When you are helping someone else, you are helping yourself**
- **People who feel rejected are hurting as bad as people with a physical injury**
- **Fear hurts as much as the real deal**

The intriguing reality is that **unlike empathy that activates only the pain network, compassion activates both the pain and the reward networks.** Let's next find a few ways to enhance our compassion.

Remove the Barriers

A patient once said to me, "I'm the only one hurting. Everyone else in the lobby seems OK." I wondered, what if every patient carries the same thought.

Most of the suffering remains unwitnessed. Perhaps you know of a family that lost a member to self-harm that no one saw coming. "He looked so happy and calm. I could never have imagined he was struggling so bad." I have heard these sad expressions several times.

The awareness that a large proportion of suffering is invisible, will help you become compassionate toward others who superficially seem like they have it all together.

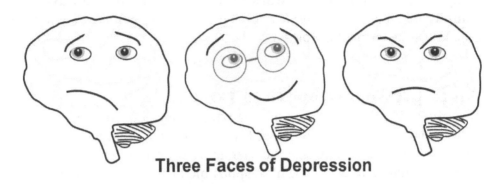

Three Faces of Depression

People feeling sad may not always look sad, because many show a brave face trying to hide their sadness

A related barrier is envy, toward someone we find more fortunate than us. Research shows when we see a wealthy person struggling, our reward network becomes active. Compelling research shows that beyond a threshold, which isn't high for most people, wealth doesn't increase happiness, takes away small daily pleasures, hurts relationships, and engenders fear. **The realization that the wealthy person is emotionally struggling as much or sometimes more than the one less fortunate can help your compassion.**

The next barrier toward compassion is fear. We find it difficult to be compassionate toward those we fear. While this is entirely understandable, it is unhelpful.

Fear puts our energy and body language in the 'prey mode' making us look vulnerable. A potential aggressor is looking out for prey (physical or emotional) and would rather not harm someone who seems self-assured. Your compassion defangs the other person, gets you out of the prey mode, and helps you get better control over your emotions, so you can take the right actions to protect yourself.

You might also feel that you really can't help the world a thousand miles away. What's the point in feeling compassion toward them? That's again a reasonable thought. It's good however to realize that your disposition not only travels farther than you think, but you also act as a role model to many. **You are a hub in a network in which you can start a wave of compassion.** You'll be surprised how far this wave can travel, sometimes touching someone half a world away.

An Expression Other than Love...

Near the end of the workday, I had an extra patient added to my calendar. I was running behind. The moment I walked into the room, he started spewing harsh words. My heart accelerated. I wanted to retaliate. I had never seen him before and wasn't responsible in any way for the issues he had with the previous care.

Nevertheless, the words that resonated in my head were, "He is going through a tough time. This is a call for help. Practice kind attention." I worked very hard on keeping my patience. He settled after a long ten minutes. What followed was a very civil discussion, problem-solving, compliments and a hug.

Cultivating this stance has taken me over a decade. Here is my brain's default—at home or work, if someone is upset, I consider it a personal attack. I assume they are trying to get me, and I need to defend myself. Not reacting right away feels passive and weak.

However, seldom has such reaction served me, my loved ones, colleagues, or others. The outcome of taking the bait—I hurt others and myself with my reaction and put everyone in a downward spiral.

A much more useful response is to remember that **a volcano spews lava because it has hot lava in its bosom**. Those upset are genuinely struggling. They aren't choosing to be this way and aren't scheming either. It's a call for help.

I can imagine such a perspective would fail with some people who have inherited a very strong genetic predisposition that squeezed the last bit of kindness out of their brain. So far, however, I have never regretted assuming that an expression other than love is indeed a call for help. Three letters that capture this perspective are—API.

API

A friend doesn't reply to your email in time, a person cuts you off on the road, someone jumps the line ahead of you, a close loved one forgets your birthday—in all these situations and more, you have a choice. You can choose to take it personally, or you can assume that the other person has good intentions but has constraints limiting them. My default is to assume negative intent and take it personally. I have learned to train myself and assume positive intent.

While **actions are important, perhaps the intentions that power the actions are even more critical.** Every single day, unintentional and unforeseen mistakes harm millions of people. We are willing to forgive these mistakes. Our rule of law also gives great importance to context and intentions. If we do not choose, however, our brain is designed to assume negative intent—an approach that hurts our present moment and creates a narrow negative view of the world.

API is not only beneficial, but it is also closer to the truth (compared to ANI—Assume Negative Intent). **In our world, the good is more common than the bad. The bad is often the wrapper that hides the good.** The good is also quickly forgotten and muffled compared to the bad.

API doesn't mean you will make yourself vulnerable. It merely means you'll keep your emotions in check, your perspective intentional, and give others benefit of doubt. You'll assume innocence. You'll recognize that like you, others have constraints that they may never share. We all are a work in progress.

Find Commonalities

Two people sit across a table for 30 minutes. They have one job to do. In this time, they have to find as many things as they can that are common between them. They come up with 48. They both have a younger sibling, had a wisdom tooth taken out, sleep on the left side, like coffee better than tea, are dog lovers, have too many passwords, been to Canada, like fiction better than nonfiction, forget flossing, haven't been to Alaska, believe in the supernatural, would like to sleep more, have failed their new year resolution, love dark chocolate, and are tired of negative news. In this short time frame, they come close to each other.

Finding commonality is one of the easiest ways to become compassionate to others. When you are flying, you can assume that everyone in the flight is crazy and unreasonable. Or you can believe that they all have similar struggles as you. I try to assume the latter and also believe they are all related to me. That perception has enhanced my every flying experience.

Often, you and others may not have the time to share your life's struggles and joys with each other. It is easiest to assume that there is a lot that is common. This simple assumption will help you feel closer and compassionate toward each other.

Celebrate Success

You just got a promotion at work. You share the good news with a colleague. Here are three possible responses:
1: "Wow! That's great news. Tell me more about your role. I want to host a party."
2: "That's great. Weren't you long due for a promotion?"
3: "Last year they offered me the same position. I declined."

The first response multiplies your joy, the second response is neutral, and the third response tries to throw cold water. Guess who will you invite more into your life, the first or the third responder?

Compassion isn't just sharing the difficult times; it is also multiplying joy. Others' success often engenders envy in us. Recognize that most people, in their moments of pleasure, feel insecure about preserving the gains and shouldering additional responsibilities that invariably accompany success. **Your ability to celebrate with others will keep you free of negative emotions, and also nurture a group of people, who will be happy in your happiness.**

Best to celebrate other's happy moments instead of throwing cold water

Compassion Fatigue

When we asked a few monks, who were traveling with His Holiness Dalai Lama about compassion fatigue, they were surprised to hear the two words—compassion and fatigue, together. In their mind, compassion is always energizing. How can it cause fatigue?

Compassionate engagement leads to fatigue if it limits itself to empathy, is associated with repeated imaginings of suffering, and has to deal with the plight of the innocent and the young. **Compassion fatigue is an important contributor to burnout**, particularly in health care. Burnout itself predisposes to greater compassion fatigue—putting the individual in a self-perpetuating loop.

Two groups of approaches can decrease compassion fatigue.

1. Increase your energy

- Think gratitude. Lower your gratitude threshold, so it includes the daily gifts that we take for granted such as access to warm water, comfortable room temperature, a refrigerator full of food, having a job, not living in a war-torn neighborhood, and more.
- Connect. Several studies show that **a strong and supportive peer group does wonders to decreasing fatigue and burnout**. Such a group can be both at the workplace as well as in personal life. Of late, researchers are looking at creating online groups of like-minded people and finding them equally beneficial.
- Think meaning. Is there a way you can connect your work, particularly dull part of your work, with something meaningful? **Finding greater purpose is the perfect antidote to fatigue and negative emotions.**
- Engage in self-care. Investing time in self-care often improves mood and sense of wellbeing much before any change in cholesterol or blood sugar numbers. **Notice what you eat, eat slower, eat healthier, avoid prolonged sitting, value and preserve your sleep, and know your numbers** (cholesterol, blood sugar, blood pressure, and others appropriate for you).
- Keep some fun time. Take out some time to enjoy your life, including pursuing an enjoyable hobby. Our goal is not only to decrease negative emotions but also enhance positive feelings.
- Cultivate a spiritual practice. The specifics of a practice depend on individual preferences and beliefs. Pick a practice that helps provide you with a broader context to your life and work, and which resonates with your belief system.

2. Decrease your energy loss

- Avoid excessive news. I believe spending several hours every day watching the news is an independent risk factor for heart disease and stroke. **Decrease your dose of daily news to the least amount necessary to keep you informed.**

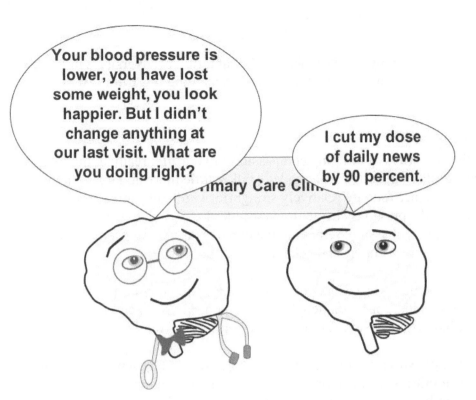

Spending too much time watching news can hurt your physical and mental wellbeing

- Lower your expectations. High expectations are a recipe for disappointment. One formula for happiness is: **Happiness = Reality - Expectations.** You can certainly change the reality, but if that doesn't seem feasible, then optimize your expectations. **Lowering expectations doesn't mean decreasing standards. It means letting go of the fruitless urge to be perfect.**

- Learn to accept. Majority of us experience at least one catastrophic event in our life. The clouds cover about two-thirds of the earth at any time. More than 80 percent of people develop back pain at some point. It won't be feasible (or, in some instances, even fair) for a person's life to be completely free of adversity, pain, or losses. Next time when faced with adversity, focus on how you can best engage and overcome it, instead of questioning its existence. With that attitude, adversity will leave a positive meaning and not a scar. Accepting this truth is wisdom.

Living it

Of the five ways of bringing compassion in your life: reading, thinking, writing, sharing, and practicing, let's talk a little more about practicing since the other four are relatively straightforward and similar to what I shared in the previous chapter on gratitude. I shared above a few ideas on practicing compassion: removing the barriers, assuming positive intent, finding commonalities, and celebrating others' success.

For practicing compassion, you can consider people in three groups: people you like (or love), people you are neutral about, and people you don't like. Compassion is most natural for people you like and love.

For people you are neutral about, I suggest starting with assuming commonalities. The person flipping burgers, driving a cab, or running a law firm has similar concerns as you. Likely all of these people are a parent, a sibling, a child, a grandparent. They have health concerns, financial concerns, worry about the future, have regrets and hurts in the past, have lost someone or something precious to them, and more. **Similar to kind attention toward strangers, you can find greater compassion by assuming the people you barely know are special and struggling, just as you are.**

People you don't like could be because they are undesirably different. Maybe they have an annoying accent, a different political view, a different perspective on climate change, or a different faith. Perhaps they don't recycle. You are unlikely to find many people whose views on every issue are completely aligned with you. We will be left with very few people if we reject everyone with views different than us.

We often have to work with people whose world views are different than us

A different group of people you don't like are those who may have actively hurt you or harbor ongoing animosity toward you. For both these groups, bringing compassion will be like lifting a mountain. I suggest starting with self-compassion.

Ask yourself—who is being hurt by harboring anger? Who is the container of negative feelings? If you aren't likely to act on your worst impulses, why not start with being kind to yourself. **Replace your negative feelings for others with compassion for the self.** Look at yourself with the eyes of the person who loves you unconditionally. Find gratitude for all that is good in your life. Accept some imperfections. Depending on your personal beliefs, give prayer a chance. Maybe someday, you might develop kind thoughts for the unreasonable others. It's OK if that day isn't today.

Before we proceed to acceptance, commit to at least one person toward whom you'll be extra kind today. If you wish, you can use one exercise from the journal, *Happier Mornings Calmer Evenings* to plan your kindness.

Today I'll be *extra* kind to... (Select at least one)

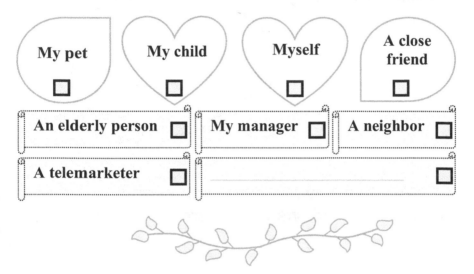

My pet ☐

My child ☐

Myself ☐

A close friend ☐

An elderly person ☐

My manager ☐

A neighbor ☐

A telemarketer ☐

_____ ☐

30. Acceptance (on Wednesdays)

Among the five principles (gratitude, compassion, acceptance, meaning, and forgiveness), I and my fellow travelers both find acceptance as the most difficult. It is because acceptance almost always applies to an undesirable experience. We don't say, "I accept that everyone loves me." We have to accept critique and insults. Acceptance also sounds passive. It is confused with apathy, giving up, becoming a doormat. Let's develop a shared understanding of acceptance as a first step.

Cute Cookies

The doorbell rings. You aren't expecting anyone. Standing at the door is an eight-year-old, with her mother waving from a few feet behind. You open the door, and the little girl says, "Hi! A box of cookies for five dollars."

This is a PR nightmare. Did you refuse to buy cookies from the little girl last evening? It's trending on Twitter.

You aren't much into cookies. What are you going to do? Shove the door in her face or buy more than you should? Most people would buy more than they should. I would do that too.

You didn't invite the girl at your front door. You don't like cookies. Nevertheless, you engage and buy them. That is acceptance.

Acceptance isn't apathy or giving up. Acceptance isn't allowing yourself to be treated like a doormat

or leaving everything to fate. **Acceptance, on the other hand, is creatively working with what is. Acceptance is empowered engagement.** Acceptance is recognizing the unpredictability of tomorrow, the asymmetries of life, realizing that we are infinitely more precious and stronger than what holds us back.

Acceptance is knowing that the only birds that can fly are the ones with asymmetric feathers. Perhaps the present challenges will eventually serve a meaning, even if that meaning isn't visible right now. Faith in the existence of such a meaning helps one see things as they are, spend less energy fighting the philosophical reason behind the asymmetries, and invest more time and resources into becoming a change agent.

Acceptance stops you from blaming "them" for your problems. Instead, you take back your locus of control, and become a change agent. You are no longer a passive bearer of the change. Acceptance is wisdom in action.

The example below will provide you with seven ingredients of acceptance.

An Annoying Allergy

Let's say each time you eat an egg product you throw up and break into hives. You are diagnosed with an egg allergy. Now at every grocery shopping, you spend 15 minutes reading labels. When you eat at a restaurant, you have to interview the chef asking for the ingredients. You can find nothing positive about this allergy. Here are the seven components of acceptance applied to this particular example.

#1. <u>Be willing to see the truth</u>: As a first step, acceptance doesn't deny the truth. **Denying or suppressing the truth seldom leads to lasting peace or happiness.** Acceptance won't claim how wonderful it is to have the allergy. Instead, acceptance lets you see the truth for what it is.

#2. <u>See the undesirable as not so terrible</u>: Next, acceptance recognizes that what seems undesirable is only a mild deviation from the normal (assuming that's what you are dealing with). It isn't as bad as it could have been. My allergy could be to twenty different food items, or it could have been an anaphylactic allergy. If the allergy is anaphylactic, acceptance, instead of lamenting on the predicament, focuses on the available options—avoidance, Epipen, desensitization, and more.

#3. <u>Contextualize the bad in the totality of life</u>: My immune system reacts to eggs but is otherwise effective at fighting infections and preventing inflammation. I also do not have any other severe illness.

Another example—Your partner loads the dishwasher like garbage can while you prefer to load it like a jewelry box. Acceptance helps you see that he or she is a great driver, always takes out the trash on time, and is terrific at keeping the backyard tidy.

#4. <u>See that the bad has an expiration date</u>: Many people with egg allergy outgrow their allergy. Children who seem like they will never become fully rational or take responsibility, outgrow their immaturity. **Acceptance sees the annoying and the imperfect as limited in time.** The same applies to many other aspects of life: **the bad in most instances has an expiration date.**

Many challenges fade with time

When experiencing the bad, instead of lifting the entire load of the future, acceptance helps you lower the load, so you live your life one hour at a time. Acceptance adds a desirable twist to the adversity, "I detest the taste of Penicillin, but I'm glad that I have to take it only for a few days."

#5. <u>See that others have similar or worse struggles</u>: Countless millions have an egg allergy. Hundreds of millions have many other allergies. Acceptance sees that my struggles are part of a common human experience. Further, acceptance asks—If most others have one or the other struggles, will it be fair if I experience no adversity? Acceptance thus is willing to share part of the burden.

#6. <u>Is it truly bad</u>? One of my loved ones has irritable bowel syndrome. He experiences daily bloating. He is also the fittest member in his family, having outlived most of his friends and relatives from his generation (he is about 86). I was thinking the other day that his bloating and early satiety could have prevented him from consuming excessive calories, thus helping his overall health. When presented with this information, he for a moment felt grateful for his bothersome symptoms. The same could apply for egg allergy and many other allergies (at least in milder forms).

#7. <u>Now that it is here, can I face it</u>? Allergies are a pain. But life goes on. In most instances, you can find ways around the allergies. **When dealing with adversity, almost always, people find greater strength and support than they think or can imagine.** Over the long term, most patients with the cancer diagnosis handle it with greater courage than they think they would or could.

Further, once past the initial shock and the rigors of the treatment, patients who have the promise of a long lifespan after the diagnosis (the definition of which is very individual) often start paying less attention to the minor annoyances. Instead, they focus on meaning, love, relationships, faith. I have met patients who in retrospect considered their cancer diagnosis as a gift, since it reset their expectations and values, and helped them appreciate their relationships much more.

I pray no human being ever has to face a diagnosis like cancer, stroke, or heart attack. However, given that more than 90 percent of us will face one or more of these or other diagnoses, it will be desirable to prepare ourselves for such an event. **Hope, courage, inspiration, and faith are strong forces that prevent the diagnoses from taking over our mind.** Acceptance is often the first step in this transformation.

You can see how **acceptance looks at the truth, sees the truth for what it is, stops catastrophizing, focuses on ways to work with the truth, and eventually may help you find meaning in the undesirable. Another way of defining acceptance is your willingness to look at the truth in its most optimistic version.**

The practice of acceptance is with the people in your life and everything else. Let's start with the people.

Accepting People

If you are like me, almost all of your friends and loved ones have annoyed you at some point. If I rejected everyone who has a loud hiccup, I would have no friends left. Implementing one or more of the above seven descriptors of acceptance can help. Here are a few ideas on how best to accept others.

Focus on what is right—Yes, they slurp while drinking coffee, but do they bring you a warm cup first thing in the morning. When you lie on a bed of flowers, you'll barely feel the petals, but the two thorns sticking in your thighs will draw the most attention. Same is with people. Remember this bias, before you choose to judge others.

Find rational context in what seems wrong—My eyes and skin are sensitive to bright lights. Even though I love the sun, I can only spend so much time outdoors. Unless I share this constraint, you might wonder why I decline most of the hiking invitations. Often, **people aren't comfortable sharing their constraints.** A kind approach will be to assume that they have a rational reason if they are wearing a woolen jacket in prickly heat.

Find meaning in what seems wrong—I once heard an interesting expression—*Thank God for my partner's imperfections. But for those imperfections, they would be with someone else!* Did your partner's 195 impatience contribute to his or her success? Is your supervisor's focus on the details the reason your product is doing so well? Did your spouse's obsession with cleaning all the surfaces prevent a flu outbreak in your home? **The higher the meaning you can find in what seems wrong, the quicker you'll be able to accept it.**

Is it truly wrong?—Sometimes we misclassify different as wrong. Our definition of right is limited to what we approve. But we have sampled such limited span of space and time. How can we always be sure what is right? While jumping into the lion enclosure in a zoo is dumb and risky, as is shoplifting or not stopping at the stop sign, many behaviors are grey. Is it OK to top off the parking meter for someone whose time has expired? Is it OK to wear the same shirt two days in a row? Is it weird if someone flosses three times a day? We often commit the fundamental attribution error—we can offer rational explanations for our behavior, but the same action from another person seems very irrational. Realizing such, you might expand your zone of "normal human behavior," making acceptance easier.

The second group of acceptance practices is for everything else—things, situations, experiences, and more. They could be only a minor issue, an intermediate issue, or a catastrophe.

Accepting Situations: Small Problems

We face small problems every day. A stalled car on a one-lane road, a moody loved one, slight headache, lost receipt,

Best to raise the threshold of what we allow to upset our equilibrium and for how long

forgotten meeting, low tire pressure, long line at the coffee shop, crowded subway, tight shoe—are just a few among countless things that can go wrong on any given day. Earlier I would let them annoy me. Now the question I ask is this—will it matter in five years?

Given that we all have finite breaths and heartbeats, we have to prioritize what we allow to influence our present-moment experience. **Anything that won't matter in five years isn't worth fretting over.** It doesn't mean you won't fix the fixable. All it means is that you won't let it penetrate your psyche and disturb your equilibrium.

One of my very comforting personal mantras is that **I won't ever get the best deal, and I am OK with it**. Every time you buy a stock, it will go down; every time you sell a stock, it will go up. Best to accept this, and of course not put all your eggs in one basket, so one stock's gyrations don't take away your peace.

Accepting Situations: Intermediate Problems

Intermediate problems are those you will likely remember in five years. A fall that broke your ankle, a pneumonia that got you into the hospital, an unexpected pink slip, a stolen wallet on an overseas trip, a broken relationship, a new diagnosis of hypertension or diabetes—these are all significant issues in life several of which will greet us on this earthly journey. A few of these and more may have already arrived in your inbox. The question is how you work with it.

I know two people who are alive today because they missed their flight. For a few hours after missing their flight, they were upset, only to realize that the computer glitch that caused them to miss the flight saved their life. I address my intermediate problems by recognizing them as a part of my human experience and assuming that they are preventing me from something much worse that I don't presently know or may never know. **An adversity could be preventing a catastrophe**. Assuming such saves the energy drain that invariably happens from thinking about the next shoe that will drop and how heavy it will be.

It will also help to **decrease expectations from humans**. "Human error" at work happens millions of times every day. Same is true for human error in relationships. At least some of it is unintentional and occurs because of ignorance, misinformation, vulnerability, and more. **Realizing that no one targeted you intentionally might numb the pain a little bit.**

Accepting Situations: Catastrophes

Most of us will experience or witness at least one catastrophe in our life. Like other adversities, disasters are also about perception. I once met a patient with advanced pancreatic cancer who was unfazed by his diagnosis, while another patient with mild osteoarthritis of her fingers was in crisis because of the perceived imperfection in her body.

I have witnessed and experienced several catastrophes: MIC gas tragedy in Bhopal, India, a good friend passing away in an accident a few hours after we had played together, a colleague taking his life, severe illness in a young child, personally dumped by my best friend as a teenager (it felt like a disaster), and a major neurologic illness as a child. Through these experiences I have realized the following:

It's OK to allow yourself to be sad. **You'll remain sad for a longer time if you try to force away sadness.**

It's OK to take help. **Those assisting you during catastrophes may not always know the right thing to do or say, but they mean well.** These are the times that can enhance your relationships.

It's OK to keep the hope. "This too shall pass" is a powerful mantra and you are not alone in experiencing such an adversity on the planet. You do not have to rush toward finding meaning but keep the hope that the meaning will manifest at some point.

It's OK to believe in the power of prayer. **In a desperate situation, prayer can offer respite, healing, hope, and for those with faith, the kind power of the divine.**

Just as there are tornado shelters in the buildings and tsunami escapes in coastal areas, it will be good to build crisis shelters for the mind. These include thoughts of the people who care about you, the meaning you have served and hope to fulfill, all that you are grateful for, inspiring role models, and the anchor of faith.

Living it

Acceptance is difficult. We confuse acceptance for apathy or giving up. Further, unlike gratitude and compassion that quickly fill us up with positive emotions, acceptance stops the drain of negative emotions. We may notice a positive effect only after some time.

The first step to practicing acceptance is to understand that it isn't giving up. **It is empowered engagement, a thoughtful and wise deployment of our finite energy.**

Start your acceptance journey with a mild annoyance, related to life's experiences or relationships. A flat tire, an unrelenting telemarketer, an elderly who repeats himself or herself, a broken windshield (assuming you have the insurance), or something else.

Use some of the principles discussed above (Will it matter in five years? Can this help me in any way? Did this annoyance prevent a catastrophe?)

Once you get comfortable with handling mild annoyances, expand your acceptance to other more difficult aspects. You'll have to be patient with yourself since the progress with acceptance is often slow. The more gratitude you can find in what is right and meaning in what seems wrong, the easier and more authentic your acceptance. Part of acceptance is prioritizing peace and happiness and pursuing a deeper meaning, instead of trying to win every argument and every battle.

You can choose to accept just because you feel loved and accepted by others

Before we move to meaning, commit to accepting one annoyance of your loved one/friend for a week and check your reason/s for accepting it.

Name of your loved one or friend:

I am willing to accept the following annoyance of my loved one or friend for a week:

My reason/s for accepting my loved one/friend's annoyance are the following (check all that apply):

I am grateful for what is right about that person	☐
I can find a rational context in what seems wrong	☐
I find meaning in what seems wrong	☐
I recognize what I call wrong may be just my own bias	☐
I believe acceptance will improve my relationships	☐

I hope you embrace acceptance, and that acceptance brings you peace and joy.

31. Meaning (on Thursdays)

World over every second five new babies arrive on our planet. The first few weeks after the childbirth are often associated with pain, sleepless nights, fatigue, fears, and more. But I have never heard a mother calling it suffering. All the discomfort is more than compensated by a sacred meaning—of bringing a precious new life into the world.

In comparison, consider another painful experience, that of passing a kidney stone. I have never heard a patient telling me, "I love this pain doctor, let it come." It is mostly because the pain of the kidney stone has no meaning. If the same patient were passing a hundred-carat diamond and needed the money, he would look forward to the pain. **Meaning changes everything.**

The Two Meanings

The meaning has two parts—the meaning of individual experience and the meaning of the totality of life.

The meaning behind an individual experience relates to how it serves us and serves the world. The experience may primarily provide pleasure (such as watching a dolphin show), may nourish our body (such as eating healthy food), or help us become a better human being (such as spending time in a church, monastery, temple, or another spiritual place, or reading an inspiring book). **Adversity can become meaningful when you find a way it has helped you become a better person or has protected you or others from a potential future adverse experience.**

The meaning of the totality of life relates to how our life serves us and the world. **A comprehensive meaning is difficult to comprehend or articulate.** Our ignorance about the full meaning is partly because we do not fully understand our place in the universe, what precedes our birth, and what follows our death. We have our beliefs and based on those beliefs our life's meaning could be realizing our faith, developing universal compassion, creating a kinder world for our planet's children, achieving enlightenment, nirvana, or another such exalted state.

I spend less time thinking about the meaning of the totality of my life. Instead, I focus on how I can make my life a little more meaningful. I do that in the context of my personal North Star.

What's the ultimate meaning of life is a difficult question to answer. An easier question is: how can I make my life more meaningful?

The North Star

In the pre-GPS era, for centuries, the north star (Polaris) helped sailors navigate the oceans. The further north the sailor reached, the higher the north star would appear. Similarly, in our lives, it helps to have a north star to navigate our journey.

My north star is the wellbeing of our children—all children. How do I make the world a better place for our planet's children—this passion drives all my efforts. My meaning helps direct my daily experiences, and also powers my life. I hope one day I realize the ultimate meaning and find that ultimate meaning directly connected to this meaning.

Spend a few minutes thinking about your personal north star, and if you wish, write it in the box below.

The Short-term and the Long-term

Minneapolis is north of Rochester and connected by highway 52N. If I am starting in Rochester and my goal is to reach Minneapolis, then taking 52S won't work. I have to align my present direction with my final destination. Similarly, **if your short-term actions don't align with your long-term meaning, then even if you succeed materially, you wouldn't be satisfied with your earthly journey.**

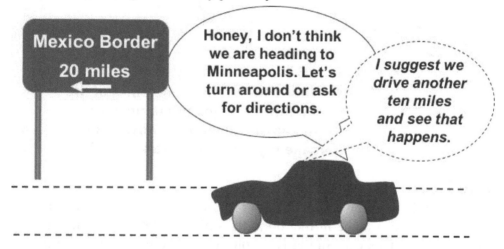

It's good to align the short-term progress to the long-term meaning, and be comfortable with asking for directions

Aligning the short-term with the long-term, while it seems obvious and straightforward, is a work of a lifetime. Because **doing the right thing day after day needs will power, self-control, patience, and confidence.** You'll also face opposition and name calling. In the school you might be called a nerd, your words may sound cheesy to some, your actions too idealistic and unreal.

But like a Lego toy with a thousand pieces, each of your righteous action will pave the way for the next part to fall in its place and contribute to the whole. Through this, you will need lots of patience, particularly if you have a good idea of how the final product should look like—your life's meaning. I can't wait for the day when all of us look at each other with kind attention and become a naturally grateful and compassionate species. I have to contend with the reality that such progress will take time. I can't force it by my sheer will power.

Forcing Meaning

Sometimes you can find a meaning behind a missed flight or spilled milk on the new sofa. But keep in mind that **the bigger the hurt, the longer it will take to find meaning**. It is extremely difficult (near impossible) to find the meaning behind a sexual assault or loss of a loved one. Forcing a meaning prematurely for self or others will be counterproductive. It will evoke anger.

Instead of meaning, in such situations, it is good to offer support and validation, without trying to contextualize the loss. It is fair to assume that **most people want validation instead of education.**

Be careful with offering gratitude to someone who is struggling. Gratitude is good at creating positive emotions, not so good with decreasing negative emotions. A mayor of a town once went to speak at a prison and spoke the following words of gratitude to the prisoners, "I am grateful you all are here to listen to me today." He didn't get a standing ovation.

Also, **be careful with investing time to reframe a problem that has an obvious solution.** If you have a thorn in one finger, it is best to take the thorn out, instead of feeling grateful that rest of the four digits aren't hurting.

One of the best ways to avoid misspeaking is to keep authentic compassion, without pity. Compassion will help you connect and speak comforting words.

The Three Questions

The three questions that can help you focus on your personal meaning are:

◊ Who am I?
◊ Why am I here?
◊ What is this world?

Likely, you have many descriptors. You are a professional, loved one, friend, colleague, neighbor, citizen, and more. **At the core, the two things that capture all your roles are service and love.** You serve others and self, and love others and self. My response to the question, who am I, is: I am an agent of service and love. **Retiring or being alone doesn't mean you can't serve and love the world.** Sending a kind note to someone is serving them. **A silent prayer for someone struggling is an expression of love.** No one can usurp this meaning from you.

The question, why am I here, is your north star. I am here to make the world a better place for our planet's children. I hope you earlier spent a few minutes thinking about your north star. If not, you can do it now. It doesn't have to be perfect or high sounding. If you are a cab driver, it could be as simple as I am here to help people reach their home safely.

Our universe is unfathomably big and complex. Trying to understand the complete physics, the chemistry, and the biology of the world is a worthy exploit but presently unachievable. A much better construct is to connect your "what" with your "why." **This world is to help support your why.** It is simultaneously a stage on which we enact the drama of our life and a school where we learn to become a wiser being. I connect the most with the idea that **the world is a giant school of learning**. We are here to learn through a rainbow of experiences. This construct helps me assume the role of a student, forever learning, embracing my ignorance and vulnerability, and thereby becoming stronger.

Living it

The search for meaning is a very personal exploration. A large part of it depends on the context. My five-year-old was in a tremendous celebratory spirit when she discovered her first loose tooth. My sixty-five-year-old patient wasn't as excited about a loose tooth.

The context depends on your experience, hopes, values, and goals. Try and answer the three questions related to your meaning below.

1. Who am I? (Imagine you were meeting an alien who knew nothing about you, your country, gender, race, faith, or even planet earth. How will you describe yourself to that person?)

2. Why am I here? (Think of your north star that inspires you into excellence)

3. What is this world? (Think of your model of the world)

The above three questions are an excellent first step to define your meaning.

As a next step answer this fundamental question:
How aligned are your short-term actions with long-term meaning?

1	2	3	4	5	6	7

Not aligned at all   Fully aligned

If your score is 4 or lower, perhaps you can do something to realign your life. Think of two changes you can make to realign your short-term actions with long-term meaning.

One thing you wish to do more of:

One thing you wish to do less of:

Finally, let's try to reframe an undesirable experience with positive meaning. Think of a mildly annoying/unwelcome experience you had during the past few weeks.

Now reframe that experience, by finding something positive in the negative (snow is the water I'll get to drink in the summer), or thinking of something worse that could have happened, but didn't.

I hope and pray you find a positive meaning every single day.

32. Forgiveness (on Fridays)

Two Feisty Sisters

I heard a version of this story many years ago.

Dorothy and Betty were two sisters who couldn't stand each other for more than a few minutes. They had learned to keep the peace by staying afar and limited their interaction to the pleasantries.

Once Dorothy got very sick with pneumonia and had to be hospitalized. She could die. Betty, the younger of the two sisters, called it a truce and took some flowers.

After the visit, as Betty was about to leave, Dorothy looked at her from behind her oxygen mask and said, "Betty if I die, I forgive you. But if I live, the fight continues!"

We don't have to be that stoic about keeping our hurts alive. Best to give forgiveness a chance before the medical resident starts reading out the advanced directive. One of the reasons we struggle with forgiveness is because we misunderstand the concept of forgiveness.

It's for You

Forgiveness isn't justifying, condoning, excusing or denying. Forgiveness is letting go of the hurts despite knowing that someone wronged you.

By forgiving, you choose to live your life by your principles. You disempower the other person's influence on your life. **You do not let those who shouldn't be in the story of your life, write the title of your story.**

Looking at it another way, you **give an eviction notice to people who inflame your brain without paying any rent.** Every single wellbeing measure—immune and inflammatory markers, heart rate variability, the risk of cardiovascular illness, happiness, sleep, relationships—improve with forgiveness. The cartoon below captures some of the benefits and a silly request from a forgiveness researcher!

With all these benefits, the next question then is—why is forgiveness so difficult?

Why Is Forgiveness So Difficult?

Imagine you are the chief of a tribe ten thousand years ago. You compete with the neighboring tribe for the same game and source of water. Last night they stole your cattle, burnt your hut, and injured your family. Would your instinct be to show the white flag and create peace? Unlikely isn't it?

For our ancestors, the options were to either fight or move the tribe to another location. Knowing who is your friend and who is your enemy was extremely important. We didn't have locked doors, security systems, and 911. We mislabeled forgiveness as weakness. Hence, we cultivated the revenge instinct.

Nature has preserved the revenge instinct in a fascinating way. Neuroscience research shows that **contemplating revenge activates the brain's reward center**. Thinking about getting even is like eating dark chocolate.

In the modern world, however, our hurts have changed. While many people still get physically assaulted, **almost all of us experience emotional hit and run nearly every week**. Our tendency to nurture the hurts and the revenge instinct compounds our problems.

Revenge Begets Revenge

In the modern world, revenge doesn't serve its purpose for two reasons:

1. Revenge doesn't douse the anger—Unlike what we might think, **revenge doesn't drench the anger fire with cool water. Instead, revenge fuels it**. This misperception of the emotional value of revenge (that we will be calm once we are even), keeps the revenge alive.

2. Revenge leads to counter revenge—If A unreasonably hurts B and B takes the revenge, then A seldom connects B's actions with his or her original insult. A considers B as unreasonable and seeks revenge against B's revenge. You can see how this will keep the cycle of assaults alive for a long time. You can see why fights amongst tribes last decades, even centuries.

Given that many of the modern hurts are emotional and overreaction to them can create catastrophic situations, and also that forgiveness is not our brain's default instinct, intentionally cultivating forgiveness is essential for lasting peace.

Three Ideas

The following three ideas will help your forgiveness journey:

1. Remove intent when you can. You were sitting on the floor when someone came from the side and pulled your cheek resulting in a small graze. Sounds like an experience that might anger you. But the perpetrator here was your ten-month-old granddaughter who crawled up to you. Very likely, you'll forgive. Because you assume that she meant no harm. The opposite of that is intentional harm by someone who tries to rob you in a parking lot. The intent in personal life as well as in law applies when a person foresees the damage that can happen from his or her action and desires to inflict such damage. **Actions with evil intent create the greatest hurts.**

To the extent it makes sense, consider that the other person didn't intend to hurt you. Perhaps they were ignorant and didn't know the consequence of their action. It's possible they acted out of fear, and you got hurt in their effort for self-protection. Maybe they aren't emotionally intelligent, have vulnerable genes, endured childhood abuse, or are going through a rough patch.

None of these thoughts are meant to say that they were right or that you will allow them to hurt you again. These thoughts are meant to soften the personal blow, so you can come closer to forgiveness, saving your energy, disempowering the other person, and putting your efforts toward self-protection and growth. If a neighbor's dog barks at you, it isn't personal. Dog's nature is to bark. Might be best to flow with it, as long as the dog is on a leash or behind a fence.

2. Find a good reason to forgive. Recall that **forgiveness is for you, not the other person**. Recognize the physical, emotional, social and occupational benefits of forgiveness. **When you forgive, you take away**

the power from the other person. **Forgiving others is an action of self-kindness**. So, if you want your good and want to be kind to yourself, choose to forgive.

3. Lift yourself in your eyes. The day we all wake up in the morning, look at the mirror, and tell the reflection with full conviction—"You are a good person. A bad thought, word, or action is unbecoming of you," will be the day we will have removed much optional suffering.

Who do you admire? What values do they embody? Start looking at yourself with the eyes of your role model. **Live your day assuming you are in the company of your role model.** The more you feel good about yourself and the higher you lift yourself in your eyes, the easier it will be for you to forgive.

The Allergy Model of Relationships

About 7 percent of us are allergic to foods, a number that seems to be rising. If you are allergic to peanuts that doesn't mean you or peanuts are independently bad. It's just that your immune system can't tolerate peanuts.

Similarly, **your mental immune system can't tolerate some people**. You may have noticed that there are some people you meet for the first time, and you feel you have known them for ages. Similarly, some people get on your nerves very quickly. Their most benign words annoy you to the core. I have a simple explanation—you are allergic to these people.

Independently, both of you might be fine. But like peanuts for peanut allergic people, these people are excellent at creating unpleasant hurtful feelings within you.

For the minor irritations, you can use the Benadryl of gratitude and compassion. For the more severe hurts, you'll need the Epipen of forgiveness. Perhaps, like allergies, a good first step is also to prevent situations where you need rescue therapy—by avoiding these people.

The advantage of the allergy model is that the constructs you use here are much less toxic compared to words like rage, hatred, jealousy, disgust, and more. Further, it softens judgments and leaves the hope for future improvement of the relationships—once they stop revving up your mental immune system and your immune system develops tolerance.

Living it

Every DIY project becomes easier if you break it down into manageable steps. The same is true for forgiveness. Here are five simple steps you can take to start your forgiveness journey.

Step 1. Pick a person you are willing to forgive. Keep in mind that people who have hurt you badly are challenging to forgive so pick only a minor hurt at this point.

Today I wish to forgive…

Step 2. Which option is better for your physical and emotional health, and relationships—choosing to forgive or harboring anger?

> I wish to forgive because…

Step 3. Soften the hurt (if it makes sense) by decreasing intentionality and if possible, finding meaning. Check if any of the following could be true.

| It is possible he/she didn't intend to hurt me | ☐ |
| It is possible this hurt could help me in the long term | ☐ |

Step 4. Lift yourself in your eyes. Check if you believe the following to be true (I hope you check both).

| The good people try to forgive | ☐ |
| I am a good person | ☐ |

Step 5. Feel inspired and decide to forgive. Start with thinking of the people you admire and those who were hurt worse than you but still chose to forgive.

> A person I admire who embodies forgiveness:
>
> A person I know who was hurt worse than me but still chose to forgive:

Check the box on the right if at this point you agree with the statement below:

In honor of the above two people, today I choose to forgive	☐

I compliment you for your effort and of course if you checked the box above, for succeeding.

Allow me to make this even easier. **In the SMART curriculum, you only have to forgive on Fridays!** Sometimes, forgiving forever is too big a commitment to make. If that applies to you, then for now, choose to forgive just on Fridays and expand as you feel appropriate and able.

Before we close, I wish to add a few additional points about forgiveness:

◊ **Forgiveness is a slow process. It won't happen in a jiffy.**

◊ **You'll often have to forgive those you feel don't deserve your forgiveness.**

◊ **Forgiveness isn't a one-time action. You'll forget you have forgiven and will have to remind yourself several times before your mind remembers it.**

◊ **Waiting for someone to seek your forgiveness will be a very long wait.**

◊ **If you aren't ready yet to forgive, take the help of gratitude and compassion.**

◊ **If you aren't sure who to be compassionate toward, practice self-compassion.**

◊ **Be very gentle to yourself and others while forgiving.** Try not to "show off" your forgiveness. For the most egregious actions, sometimes verbalizing that you have forgiven helps. In many situations, it is best to show your forgiveness only by your behavior (engagement, kindness).

◊ All the ideas above apply to self-forgiveness. **Self-forgiveness helps with forgiving others; forgiving others helps with self-forgiveness.**

Sometimes people who hurt us may not even know they did, or pretend ignorance

Even if you failed at your first forgiveness attempt, keep the pilot fire alive. Research shows your intention to forgive is good enough to enhance your daily happiness, and free your brain's real estate to continue making positive changes, such as picking good habits. That's where we are going next.

33. Pick One

Earlier I invited you to drop one unhealthy habit. We chose prolonged sitting, excessive multitasking, and overdosing on the daily news. Now we will pick one healthy habit by exercising your most powerful gift—the power to choose.

The number one cause of premature death in the U.S. is people's inability to make good choices. Good choices not only change your physical body, but they also favor expression of the healthier genes, putting you into as some researchers call, an upward spiral of life.

The three core domains of wellness are diet, exercise, and sleep. I am sure you have access to great information about all three. Here I will spend a few paragraphs with diet and briefly touch upon exercise and sleep.

Diet

The four aspects of intelligent and healthy food intake are: slow, small, savor, and smart.

Slow: Unlike the broadband connection between the heart and the brain, the link between the stomach and the brain is like the old 56k, and at times clunky. **It takes 10-20 minutes for the brain to register the stomach's fullness.** On a day you are eating 40 calories a minute, you will consume north of extra 400 calories before you get the signal to stop. The result—you might have to loosen your belt before you leave the table.

Growing up I learned that we should chew each bite at least the number of times we have teeth in our mouth i.e., 32 times. **When you chew thoroughly and eat slowly, you get timely feedback from the brain.** You stop when you feel comfortably full, to find yourself pleasantly full in 10 minutes.

Small: The digestion starts in the mouth with the help of the saliva. **Take small deliberate bites and help your stomach with your mouth.** The same slice eaten in four bites may not satisfy your hunger forcing you to eat more, compared to twelve morsels that will lead to greater joy and satisfaction, and lower long-term calorie consumption.

Savor: Research shows **a lot of our eating is automatic—happening beyond our conscious awareness.** We stop eating not because we are full, but because the TV program we were watching got over. The bigger the bowl, the higher the food consumption, even the stale and tasteless options.

Our eating is often beyond our conscious awareness

The key to savoring food is to notice what you are eating. Notice the color, shape, and fragrance. Spend quality time with the people sharing your table. **Avoid fast-paced television or cluttered kitchen—both increase caloric intake.**

The more you notice your food and savor it, the fewer calories you consume. **In research, people who could remember their lunch ate less during the rest of the day.**

Smart: If your body were the most expensive luxury car, what kind of fuel would you fill? Would you pick third-grade fuel or the best quality? I am sure your answer is the latter. The same applies to your food since your body indeed is better than an ultra-luxury car.

Eat fresh, contaminant-free, low calorie-density food. We eat about the same amount of food (3-4 pounds) each day. That much raw vegetables would be about 400 calories, while cheese would be 10,000 calories. Hence the reason to make wiser selections.

Smart choices don't mean eating steamed broccoli three times a day. You'd have to start an anti-nausea pill in a week if you did that. Smart choices mean creating the right mix of mostly low calorie-density with a small amount of high calorie-density food. To me, that is eating smart.

When I was young, my mother always said—fill a third of your stomach with food, a third with water, and the rest with air. I am sure I wasn't too excited with that proposal then, but now I can see the wisdom behind that teaching.

Exercise

Think of anything good you want in life—physical health, emotional health, success at work, better relationships, longer life—all of that is more likely if you live an active life. Many of us, however, find little time during the day for exercise. Instead of being physically active and mentally relaxed, we are often mentally active and physically relaxed.

Here are three quick ideas about exercise:
◊ **Instead of waiting for the ideal 45-minute workout, try to fit in micro workouts multiple times during the day** (such as climbing four flights of stairs, five-minutes of jump rope, few yoga asanas).

◊ Make exercise fun (such as tennis, group martial arts, Zumba).

◊ Partner with your spouse, best friend, colleague or someone who will help you create the routine and hold you mutually accountable.

Sleep

The following line might wake you up—*in research a good model of an older brain is a young brain that hasn't slept well.* Sleep clears the brain of the chemicals accumulated during its metabolic activity throughout the day. A particular network of channels opens during the night (called the glymphatic channels) that act as garbage trucks for the brain. Inadequate sleep causes these chemicals to accumulate leading to nerve damage.

About half of us aren't getting good quantity or sound quality sleep, often both. Here are a few thoughts about sleep:

◊ If you do not sleep for enough number of hours, the problem is simple—to make sure you are in bed for the prescribed time. Prioritize your sleep if you wish to keep your brain and heart healthy, maintain good focus, and not increase the risk of accidents.

◊ If your sleep quality isn't good, get to the bottom of your problem as you would if your blood pressure was 220/100. **In many instances poor sleep may be coming from unresolved stress or anxiety, creating a circular loop.**

Sleep apnea, chronic pain, medication side effects, noisy environment are some other medically addressable causes. Consult a sleep specialist who will know how to measure the quality and quantity of your sleep and is able to help you find a reversible cause.

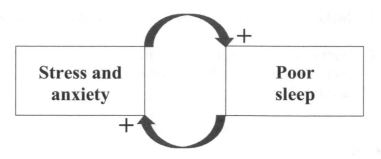

**Stress disrupts sleep and lack
of sleep predisposes to stress**

◊ A small proportion of us have a primary sleep disorder. Your sleep specialist should be able to diagnose if that is the case and provide appropriate treatment.

◊ Often, sleep issues tend to be long lasting and don't have an easy fix. Add ten to twenty minutes of deep breathing practice (such as with calm and energize meditation, other practices on myhappinesspal.com or several other excellent websites and apps). I speculate that deep breathing with lower adrenaline in the blood might open the same channels and clear your brain, though this research isn't entirely conclusive yet.

Of the three core wellness domains, pick one where you feel the need and potential for improvement, and see how you can make at least a 10 percent improvement in one of them.

I feel the need and potential for the most significant improvement in my:

Diet	☐
Exercise	☐
Sleep	☐

Write the first step you are willing to take to improve your wellness.

Before we close this chapter, I invite you to note these three numbers and if you aren't sure, find them from your health care provider's office: Your Total and LDL cholesterol, Blood Glucose, Blood pressure.

If the numbers aren't optimal them think about what lifestyle changes can bring them in the desired range.

34. Inspiration

Allow me to ask you a question that I request you to answer in ten seconds.

Who or what is inspiring you today?

If it took you more than ten seconds to think about a person or meaning that is inspiring you right now, your day will not be filled with as much energy and joy as it could be.

What is Inspiration?

An inspired state is one of uplifting energy that fills you with the drive and vision to do or create something phenomenal. Inspiration lifts your entire being and helps you go beyond yourself.

Inspiration also gives you great clarity about what is important and worthy of your time. You lose all selfishness in this state, and rise above yourself, focusing on internal mastery rather than outdoing the competition.

Such an internally motivated state is essential to achieving your highest potential and creating excellence. Research shows that authors who feel inspired in their writing are judged by their readers to be more creative, and the more inspired you are higher the number of your patents.

What inspires a person tends to be very individual and depends not only on what you seek but also on your age and the stage of your life. Broadly, there are two types of inspirations—by and to—both taking you to this higher state.

By and To

You can be inspired *by* a person or inspired *to* do something spectacular.

I felt inspired by reading the story of Marie Curie. One of my earliest inspirations was seeing a movie (Boot Polish), where a young orphan boy dreams about polishing people's shoes so well that his clients start seeing their faces in their boots. This little boy's passion, innocence, and the dignity of labor inspired me. Sister Mary Joseph of Mayo Clinic, who as a nurse described a physical sign that helped physicians diagnose pancreatic cancer inspired me. I was also inspired by a janitor who I found embodied an authentic and kind presence and a tremendous sense of humor. Each of these people inspire me with their excellence.

The second type of inspiration, which is feeling inspired to do something spectacular more directly leads you to action. Seeing the plight of soldiers injured in the war inspired Henry Dunant to create the International Red Cross. From Mother Teresa to Albert Einstein, Isaac Newton to Nikolai Tesla—**every person who has made a transformative contribution to the world found inspiration by observation, a life event, or a meaning.**

My small contribution started when I felt inspired to search for the cause of the disconnect between material and emotional wellbeing and find ways to end optional stress and suffering on the planet.

Transformative Inspirations

Inspirations may or may not have a meaning. The most mature and transformative inspirations draw their energy from a reason that we call, meaning. Whether that meaning is stopping ivory trade, slowing climate change, eliminating homelessness, nuclear disarmament, world peace, or more, the main connecting link among all these meanings is achieving something higher than oneself. These meanings are altruistic. The inspired serving these meanings have transcended the need for recognition or accolades.

Often, inspirations that happen at a young age, when we are more focused on self and haven't developed a world-centric view, aren't governed by meaning. Such inspirations, however, till the soil for a later age, meaning-driven inspirations.

In general, **meaning provides the why and inspiration helps with the what.** You need a combination of the two to climb to excellence.

Micro-inspirations

The life-changing inspirations that redirect the entire trajectory of your life happen only occasionally. They also can't be willed. You can, however, choose to find micro-inspirations on most days. Such a pursuit not only will lift your day, but also keep you prepared for the life-changing inspiring event.

Finding micro-inspirations will need more profound presence and deeper thinking. I look for these inspirations on most days—in physical form or stories. The evergreens inspire me as they withstand the cold; the perennials inspire me as they park all their energy in their roots in the winter and sprout again in the spring.

I am inspired by the octopus moms that protect their eggs for six months without moving or eating, by the honey bees that work non-stop serving their hive, by **children with disability who focus on their abilities and come to the school each day with a smile and a can-do attitude**, by nurses who work all night with remarkable patience, by firefighters who run toward the

Ms. B, please don't sting me. You are one of my inspirations. Honest!

blaze while everyone is running away from it. If you choose, every single day you can find a person or an experience that can inspire you.

Your day could be a downer, an average day, a day you are engaged, in flow, or inspired. Let's convert your today into a day of inspiration. Write below five people, experiences, or entities that you find inspiring.

1.

2.

3.

4.

5.

Pick one person or idea from the list you produced and see how you can implement that idea into your life today.

I hope you spend many days of your life engaged, in flow, and inspired.

35. Summary

The four core practices that constitute the SMART program are noted below.

> **Core practice #1: First thing in the morning, think about five people in your life who mean a lot to you and send them your silent gratitude.**

> **Core practice #2: Give two minutes of undivided attention to at least one person each day who deserves that attention but isn't presently getting it.**

> **Core practice #3: Choose to send a silent good wish to as many people as you can during the day.**

> **Core practice #4: Align your day with one or more of the five principles—gratitude, compassion, acceptance, meaning, and forgiveness.**

In addition, I have shared the following suggestions:
◊ **Dropping one (or more) unhealthy habit (prolonged sitting, habitual multitasking, or a daily dose of excessive news)**
◊ **Sitting meditation practice**
◊ **Picking one (or more) healthy habit (healthy diet, exercise, sleep)**
◊ **Finding inspiration (*by* someone or *to* do something)**

Fully integrating all of these ideas in your life will take some time. Initially, you'll need reminders, discipline, and intentional effort. After a few months, the practices will become increasingly effortless. Consider working along with the accompanying *The Resilience Journal* that'll help you create the discipline and keep track of your progress.

I'll complete module IV with summarizing the following key learning points:
1. Our brain is by design a conflicted organ
2. Practice the five principles to redirect your thinking
3. Make one positive change in your diet, exercise, and sleep
4. Whenever you can live your day feeling inspired

Our brain is by design a conflicted organ
Our brain is the most complex information processor ever built. It integrates large volumes of information with personal preferences and values, past experiences, and anticipated future, to come with cohesive words and actions. It also coordinates, and in some instances directs, a multitude of functions including blood circulation, breathing, maintenance of posture, registering sensations, endocrine function, immune function, and more. The brain also has to learn and adapt to changing environments almost every single day.

Every good action, however well meaning, can have unintended adverse consequences, causing conflicts in our brain

Further, the brain has to

prioritize. **What is good for one body part may not be suitable for another.** Running can help the heart but hurt the knees. Aspirin can keep the coronaries clean but cause bleeding and stomach ulcers. The brain thus has to integrate conflicting input coming from the outside world as well as its own thoughts. Neuroscientists are still investigating where and how all this input converges to create a cohesive response.

In this effort, the brain, despite its awesomeness, is still a student. Its neurons misfire. It misjudges. It forgets. It has limited attention. It can't think of the very long term. It overlooks its values, feels unworthy and lonely. Hence my conclusion that I can't rely on my brain to consistently think rational thoughts. I need principles that I can trust, which are validated by science, acceptable to large swathes of humanity, and have been around for a long time. These are the principles of gratitude, compassion, acceptance, meaning, and forgiveness.

Practice the five principles to redirect your thinking

I tried to anchor my thoughts, words, and actions in one or two principles. I tried compassion and then gratitude. But alone they didn't work. I realized that **given the complexity of mine and most human's life, we need a set of principles that can capture the richness of our existence.** Hence the five principles.

Gratitude, compassion, acceptance, meaning, and forgiveness have been around for thousands of years and will be here as long as humanity survives. They have been tested and found valuable by science. Each of these principles engages the higher cortical brain and soothes the lower limbic areas. Together, they offer a powerful GPS to direct the flow of life. They are like the five fingers of the hand, that together are greater than the sum of their parts.

I have offered a daily approach through anchoring the principle to a day of the week, and the five ways of bringing these principles in your life through reading, thinking, writing, sharing, and practicing. The main idea is to lower your threshold for practicing these principles and create a daily discipline.

When in doubt you can go back to gratitude and compassion because one or both of them will be relevant for almost every life situation. Keep in mind that the suggestions here are just a starter kit. With practice, you'll deepen your understanding, and if you have an anchor of faith, will find ways to integrate these principles with your faith. **A combination of these principles, the neuroscience, and faith can be a powerful transformative force to change your life completely.**

Make one positive change in your diet, exercise, and sleep

When you buy a car, you keep it serviced, oils changed, tires rotated, and so on. The same vehicle, if unkempt, will wear out at 50,000 miles versus running for 200,000. The same applies to our physical body. Our average lifespan is almost three times that of a person living a thousand years ago. Many of our body systems need maintenance to keep their smooth functioning. Some of these you can't influence, such as the gallbladder. But many you can help—such as your heart, your muscles, your skin, and of course your brain.

The three activities—diet, exercise and sleep, affect every part of the body. **The world is presently colluding to push you into unhealthy eating, sedentary lifestyle, and non-restorative sleep. You'll have to take charge, all the while remembering that lasting changes take considerable effort.**

Hence, instead of all three, pick one of the domains that you feel needs the most significant help and where you feel most capable of changing. Make a small change, integrate it in your life, and then move forward with a bigger difference.

If you move a ship's direction by three degrees, a thousand miles later, the ship reaches an entirely different place. The same applies to your life. **Even a small change, when sustained, becomes transformative. The best time to start that change is today. Postponing to tomorrow will be too late and will likely lead to a delay of ten years or more.**

Whenever you can, live your day feeling inspired

Based on our current lifespan, we live about 30,000 days. Your day could be a downer, an average day, a day you are engaged, in flow, or inspired. The higher the proportion of the days that you feel inspired, the more meaningful and enjoyable your life.

The most profound transformative inspirations are spontaneous. You can't will them. They motivate you internally, infuse you with energy, make you selfless, driving you toward mastery. **The smaller micro-inspirations can be pursued intentionally.** I invite you to seek micro-inspirations on most days, so your days are uplifted, and you are ready for those rare moments of inspirations that come unannounced.

Find a little inspiration from the trees, from the water in your faucet, a colony of ants, a pack of wildebeest in a nature program, honeybees, the seven wonders of the world, the vulnerable patients, the honest

Our mind has a tendency to forget and thus needs frequent reminders

citizens, and more. Find inspiration also from the sayings of the poets, philosophers, and contemplatives you admire. Be inspired by the teachings of your faith.

And on days you completely forget to practice one of these principles, remember that **forgetting is the very nature of the human mind.** We need frequent reminders, even to be happy.

Thank you for living an inspired life that helps us together build a kinder and more hopeful world for our planet's children.

V

SMART RESEARCH & ATTRIBUTES

SMART has been adapted to a number of populations. While the core construct remains the same, the program is customized to the particular challenges that are unique to a particular subgroup. We have tested these adaptations in about 30 clinical trials. This section shares some of the research, the core idea around the adaptations, and the distinguishing attributes of the SMART program.

36. SMART Research

So far, we have tested SMART in about 30 clinical trials with promising evidence of efficacy for several conditions without any adverse effects.

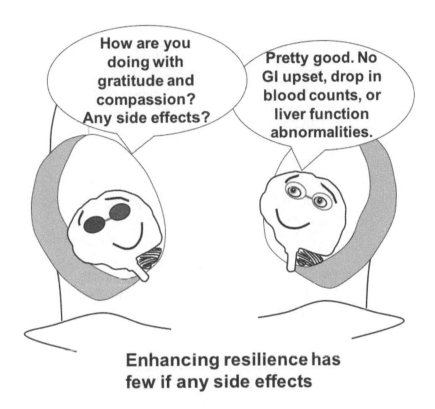

Enhancing resilience has
few if any side effects

The following summarizes the individual studies with a very succinct description of the results. The details here are adapted from the website resilientoption.com.

Completed Clinical Trials:

1. Sood A, Prasad, K, Schroeder D, Varkey P. Stress management and resilience training among Department of Medicine faculty: a

pilot randomized clinical trial. J Gen Intern Med. 2011 Aug;26(8):858-61.

In this randomized clinical trial, a brief training to enhance resilience and decrease stress among physicians led to a statistically significant improvement in resilience, stress, anxiety, and overall quality of life.

2. Loprinzi CE, Prasad K, Schroeder DR, Sood A. Stress Management and Resilience Training (SMART) program to decrease stress and enhance resilience among breast cancer survivors: a pilot randomized clinical trial. Clin Breast Cancer. 2011 Dec;11(6):364-8.

A brief, predominantly group-based resilience training intervention in patients with breast cancer led to a statistically significant lowering of stress and anxiety and improvement in the quality of life and resilience, in a randomized clinical trial.

3. Sood A, Sharma V, Schroeder DR, Gorman B. Stress Management and Resiliency Training (SMART) program among Department of Radiology faculty: a pilot randomized clinical trial. Explore (NY). 2014 Nov-Dec;10(6):358-63.

A single 90-minute session followed by two brief phone calls to decrease stress among radiologists using the SMART program, significantly improved anxiety, stress, quality of life, and mindful attention. Resilience also improved but the change was not statistically significant.

4. Chesak SS, Bhagra A, Schroeder DR, Foy DA, Cutshall SM, Sood A. Enhancing resilience among new nurses: feasibility and efficacy of a pilot intervention. Ochsner J. 2015 Spring;15(1):38-44.

Integrating a Stress Management and Resiliency Training (SMART) program within an employee orientation for nurses helped increase mindfulness and resilience scores and decrease stress and anxiety.

5. Stonnington CM, Darby B, Santucci A, Mulligan P, Pathuis P, Cuc A, Hentz JG, Zhang N, Mulligan D, Sood A. A resilience intervention involving mindfulness training for transplant patients and their caregivers. Clin Transplant. 2016 Nov;30(11):1466-1472.

A six-week mindfulness-based resilience training (MBRT) class that incorporated mindfulness practice, yoga and neuroscience of stress and resilience significantly improved perceived stress, depression, anxiety, positive and negative affect, and mental quality of life among transplant patients and their caregivers.

6. Sharma V, Sood A, Prasad K, Loehrer L, Schroeder D, Brent B. Bibliotherapy to decrease stress and anxiety and increase resilience and mindfulness: a pilot trial. Explore (NY). 2014 Jul-Aug;10(4):248-52.

A brief, self-directed resilience program provided a statistically significant improvement in resilience, mindfulness, and quality of life, and lower stress and anxiety at 12-weeks.

7. Magtibay DL, Chesak SS, Coughlin K, Sood A. Decreasing Stress and Burnout in Nurses: Efficacy of Blended Learning with Stress Management and Resilience Training Program. J Nurs Adm. 2017 Jul/Aug;47(7-8):391-395.

A combined web-based and in-person Stress Management and Resiliency Training (SMART) program led to statistically significant decrease in anxiety, stress, and burnout and increase in resilience, happiness, and mindfulness among a group of nurses.

8. Werneburg B, A; Sarah M. Jenkins, MS; Jamie L. Friend, BS; Bridget E. Berkland, MA; Matthew M. Clark, PhD; Jordan K. Rosedahl, BS; Heather R. Preston, MS; Denise C. Daniels, BS; Beth A. Riley, MBA; Kerry D. Olsen, MD; Amit Sood, MD. Improving Resiliency in Health Care Employees. American Journal of Health Behavior.

   A 12-week training in stress management and resilience led to statistically significant improvement in resiliency, perceived stress, anxiety level, quality of life, and health behaviors at the end of the intervention and further three-months follow up.

9. Bridget E. Berkland, MA, Brooke L. Werneburg, BA, Sarah M. Jenkins, MS, Jamie L. Friend, BS, Matthew M. Clark, PhD, Jordan K. Rosedahl, BS, Paul J. Limburg, MD, Beth A. Riley, MBA, Denise R. Lecy, BS, Amit Sood, MD. Improving Happiness, Life Satisfaction and Gratitude in Health Care Workers: A Worksite Wellness Intervention. Mayo Clinic Proceedings.

   In health care workers, training in a resilience program (SMART) resulted in statistically significant improvements in happiness, satisfaction with life, gratitude, resilience, mindfulness, and spirituality.

10. Prasad K, Wahner-Roedler DL, Cha SS, Sood A. Effect of a single-session meditation training to reduce stress and improve quality of life among health care professionals: a "dose-ranging" feasibility study. Altern Ther Health Med. 2011 May-Jun;17(3):46-9

A paced breathing intervention for 15 minutes once or twice a day after a single training session improved stress, anxiety, and quality of life among health care employees.

11. Kashani K, Carrera P, De Moraes AG, Sood A, Onigkeit JA, Ramar K. Stress and burnout among critical care fellows: preliminary evaluation of an educational intervention. Med Educ Online. 2015 Jul 23;20:27840.

    Two out of three (67%) critical care fellows who participated in a single, 90-minute stress management session adapted from the Stress Management and Resiliency Training (SMART) program reported strengthened ability to deal with stressful situations. The study didn't find significant improvement in self-reported burnout.

12. Chesak, Sherry PhD, RN; Morin, Karen, PhD, RN, ANEF, FAAN ; Cutshall, Susanne DNP, APRN, CNS; Sarah Jenkins, MS; Sood, Amit MD, MSc. Feasibility of Integrating a Resiliency Training in a Nurse Residency Program: A Controlled Trial with Long-Term Follow-up. (Poster presented; PhD thesis defended; Manuscript submitted)

    Integration of a Stress Management and Resiliency Training (SMART) program within a pilot nurse residency program led to statistically significant improvement in stress, mindfulness, and resilience within the intervention group, compared to a control group of nurses that received no such training.

13. Laura D. Steinkraus, Barbara L. Joyce, PhD, Amit Sood, MD MSc Integration of Stress Management and Resilience Training (SMART) Program Among Medical Students: A Pilot Study. (Poster presented; Manuscript in preparation)

    In this single-arm study, SMART program taught by a medical student to other students led to statistically significant improvement in mindfulness and anxiety up to one year of follow up.

14. Zaraq Khan MBBS; Debbie L. Fuehrer LPCC; Richa Sood MD, Charles C. Coddington MD; Gaurang S. Daftary MD, Jessica L. Bleess PA-C; Elizabeth A. Stewart MD; Jani R. Jensen MD; and Amit Sood MD. Stress Management and Resilience Training (SMART) therapy for couples undergoing in vitro fertilization (IVF): A Randomized Controlled Trial (RCT) (Poster presented; Manuscript in preparation)

Among couples undergoing IVF, training in brief SMART program, compared to a control group, led to significant improvement in generalized and fertility-related anxiety. Both men and women responded to the intervention.

15. Sherry S. Chesak, PhD, RN, Anjali Bhagra, MD, Sarah M. Jenkins, MS, Amit Sood, MD. Stress Management and Resilience Training for Public School Teachers and Staff: A Novel Intervention to Enhance Resilience and Positively Impact Student Interactions. (Manuscript submitted)

In a clinical trial involving public school teachers and staff, SMART training led to statistically significant improvement in participant anxiety (P<.001); gratitude (P=.005); and quality of life (P<.001). Most participants reported that the skills learned positively affected interactions with students (77.2%) and coworkers (72.2%).

16. Jose R Medina Inojosa MD, Mariana Garcia MD, Sharon L. Mulvagh MD, Saswati Mahapatra MS, Francisco Jimenez-Lopez MD, Brent A Bauer MD, Stephen S Cha, Amit Sood MD, Anjali Bhagra MD. Stress Management and Resilience Intervention in Women's Heart Clinic: a Pilot Clinical Trial. (Poster presented; Manuscript submitted)

In this clinical trial among patients at women's heart clinic, both in person and online training in the SMART program led to statistically significant improvement in perceived stress and anxiety and significant improvement in depressive symptoms among patients with higher depressive symptoms.

17. Dyrbye LN, Shanafelt TD, Werner L, Sood A, Satele D, Wolanskyj AP. The Impact of a Required Longitudinal Stress Management and Resilience Training Course for First-Year Medical Students. J Gen Intern Med. 2017 Aug 31

Integration of a required mindfulness-based stress management course in the curriculum of first-year medical students did not lead to significant improvements in medical student well-being or empathy.

18. Gnagey, A, Cutshall S, Sood A. Impact of a Pilot Wellness Curriculum on Healthy Behaviors, Resilience, Stress, Burnout, and Anxiety among Student Registered Nurse Anesthetists. (Poster presented, Master's thesis defended, Manuscript in preparation)

Integration of stress management and resilience training among nurse anesthetists was associated with significant improvement in stress and burnout symptoms in the cohort that participated in the training.

19. Dhanorker S, Kamath J, Shanafelt T, Sood, A. Reducing Burnout by Enhancing Resiliency. Journal of Health Care Management. 2018

In this worksite intervention among engineering and consulting professionals training in stress management and resilience skills led to a statistically significant decrease in burnout with qualitative feedback supportive of the efficacy of the program.

241

20. Sharma V, Saito Y, Sood A. SMART program for patients with IBS. (Master's in Clinical Research thesis defended with this study)

In this randomized clinical trial, training in SMART program led to a significant improvement in anxiety, satisfaction with life and gratitude, while the control arm that received stress management DVD had no significant changes.

21. West, R.R., Lauver, D. R., & Sood, A. Mindfulness skills training for stress management among low socioeconomic workers. (PhD thesis defended with this study; Several posters presented)

In this randomized trial involving low-income migrant workers, compared to a control group that received nutrition education, training in stress management and resilience skills was associated with improvement in stress and mindfulness, with qualitative data supporting the quantitative outcome.

22. Gullickson A, Graham MA, Amundson KA, Smyth KT, Sood A. A mindfulness and neuroscience-based intervention: Stress management and resilience in the workplace. (Master's thesis defended with this study)

In this qualitative study, participation in stress management and resilience training program was associated with participants' orientation to time, self-care, relationships with clients and coworkers, and improved coping skills within the work environment.

23. Fuehrer D, Schroeder D, Sood A. SMART Program: Outcomes of Train-the-Trainer program.

Participants in the SMART train-the-trainer program experienced statistically significant improvement in resilience, stress, anxiety, and quality of life.

24. Seshadri A, Clark MM, Jeanson K et al. Stress Management and Resiliency Training (SMART)in Depressed Patients: A Feasibility Study. Manuscript submitted for publication.

   In this clinical trial involving 23 participants, 8 weeks of SMART training was associated with significant improvement in resilience, stress, and depression.

Clinical Trials (Ongoing)

25. Sex SMART—This study is assessing the efficacy of resilience training among couples with intimacy issues.
   (Study completed. Results being analyzed)

26. Patients with melanoma—This study is assessing the efficacy of resilience training for stress and wellbeing measures and immune markers among patients with melanoma.

27. Effect on Brain Networks—This study is assessing the effect of resiliency training on the organization of brain networks in healthy adults.
   (Study completed. Results being analyzed)

28. Employee populations—Several studies are assessing the efficacy of resiliency training among different employee populations for wellbeing measures, productivity, and resilience.

29. SMART for IBS—This study is assessing the efficacy of SMART among patients with IBS at UCLA.

30. SMART for Physicians—This study is assessing the efficacy of online SMART program among physicians at the University of Ottawa, Canada.

Observational Studies

1. Clark MM, Jenkins SM, Hagen PT, Riley BA, Eriksen CA, Heath AL, Vickers Douglas KS, Werneburg BL, Lopez-Jimenez F, Sood A, Benzo RP, Olsen KD. High Stress and Negative Health Behaviors: A Five-Year Wellness Center Member Cohort Study. J Occup Environ Med. 2016 Sep;58(9):868-73.

   In this study, high-stress levels were associated with negative health behaviors, such as low physical activity and poor nutritional habits, as well as lower mental health and perceived overall health among a group of employees at an academic medical center.

2. Leppin AL, Bora PR, Tilburt JC, Gionfriddo MR, Zeballos-Palacios C, Dulohery MM, Sood A, Erwin PJ, Brito JP, Boehmer KR, Montori VM. The efficacy of resiliency training programs: a systematic review and meta-analysis of randomized trials. PLoS One. 2014 Oct 27;9(10):e111420.

   This study reviewed and compiled the currently known resiliency programs in a systematic review.

3. Sood A, Jones DT. On mind wandering, attention, brain networks, and meditation. Explore (NY). 2013 May-Jun;9(3):136-41.

   This highly cited review article provides a mechanistic understanding of meditation in the context of recent advances in neurosciences about mind wandering, attention, and brain networks.

4. Kermott C, Jenkins S, Sood A. A survey of corporate executives and their spouses.

   In this large study involving over 2000 participants, our team has found that resilience correlates with better physical health, emotional wellbeing, deeper relationships and greater success at work. (Several manuscripts in preparation)

Published Books
1. *The Mayo Clinic Guide to Stress-Free Living.* Sood, A
2. *The Mayo Clinic Handbook for Happiness.* Sood, A
3. *Immerse: A 52-week Course in Resilient Living.* Sood, A
4. *Mindfulness Redesigned for the Twenty*-First Century. Sood, A
5. *The Resilience Journal.* Sood, A
6. *Stronger: The Science and Art of Stress Resilience.* Sood, A
7. *Happier Mornings Calmer Evenings.* Sood, A
8. *SMART with Dr. Sood.* Sood, A

Completed Master's and PhD Thesis
1. Gullickson A.M. Attention and Interpretation Training in a Community-Based Mental Health Agency. Masters in Social Work Clinical Research Committee, Saint Catherine University/University of Saint Thomas School of Social Work, 2011.
2. West R. R. Brief mindfulness skills training intervention among low SES workers. PhD Thesis, University of Illinois at Chicago, 2011.
3. Voigt B. The Impact of Attention and Interpretation Therapy (AIT) on the Practitioner: Beneficial for Helping Professionals? Master's thesis, St. Catherine University 2013.
4. Chesak S. Attention and Interpretation Therapy Among Newly Hired Nurses. PhD Thesis, University of Wisconsin-Milwaukee.
5. Sharma V., M.D. SMART Program for Irritable Bowel Syndrome. Masters in Clinical Research, Mayo Clinic Rochester.
6. Gnagey, A. Impact of a Pilot Wellness Curriculum on Healthy Behaviors, Resilience, Stress, Burnout, and Anxiety among Student Registered Nurse Anesthetists. Doctoral thesis, Mayo Clinic Rochester.

Abstracts / Posters (List last updated: 2014)

1. Gullickson A. M., Graham M. A., Amundson K.A., Smyth K. T., Sood A. A Mindfulness and Neuroscience Based Intervention: Stress Management and Resilience in the Workplace. Poster session at the meeting of the International Symposia of Contemplative Studies, Denver, Colorado, April 2012.
2. West R., Lauver D., Sood A. Mindfulness skills training for stress management among low socioeconomic workers. Midwest Nursing Research Society 36th Annual Research Conference, Dearborn, Michigan, April, 2012.
3. Sood A. Stress Management and Resilience Training (SMART) Program to Decrease Stress and Enhance Resilience Among Breast Cancer Survivors: A Randomized Trial. 2012 International Research Congress on Integrative Medicine and Health, Portland, Oregon, May 15–18, 2012.
4. Sood A. Stress Management and Resilience Training among Department of Medicine Faculty: A Pilot Randomized Clinical Trial. 2012 International Research Congress on Integrative Medicine and Health, Portland, Oregon, May 15–18, 2012.
5. Sharma V, Sood A. Self Help Intervention to Decrease Stress and Increase Mindfulness: A Pilot Trial. 2012 International Research Congress on Integrative Medicine and Health, Portland, Oregon, May 15–18, 2012.
6. West, R. R., Lauver, D.R., & Sood A. Enhancing study recruitment and retention among community- based low socioeconomic workers. 19th National Evidence-based Practice Conference, Iowa, City, IA, May 3–4, 2012.
7. Chesak S., Foy D., Cutshall S., Sood A. A Stress Management and Resiliency Training (SMART) Program for Newly Hired Nurses. 2012 AHNA Annual Conference. Snowbird, UT, June 2012.
8. West, R, Lauver, D, Sood A. Strategies to improve recruitment and retention among a sample of low socioeconomic workers. Midwest Nursing Research Society 36th Annual Research Conference, Dearborn, Michigan, April 12–15, 2012.
9. Chesak, S, Sood, A, Morin, K, Cutshall, S, Douglas, KV, Ridgeway, J. Integration of A Stress Management and Resiliency Training (SMART) Program in a Nurse ResidencyProgram: A Feasibility Study. The Journal of Alternative and Complementary Medicine. May 2014, 20(5): A101-A101.

doi:10.1089/acm.2014.5267. Published in Volume: 20 Issue 5:
May 7, 2014
http://online.liebertpub.com/doi/pdfplus/10.1089/acm.2014.5267.a
bstract

37. SMART Customized

I was a different species as a second grader. As a medical student, my concerns and hopes were very different from what they are today.

Similarly, the stressors facing a partner in a New York law firm are often very different compared to the stressors of a caregiver who is living in rural Idaho with her mother who has advanced dementia. Nevertheless, at a basic human level, we are all very similar.

SMART thus has to be customized to the individual group yet offer a set of insights and skills that resonate with the majority. The integration of universal appeal with customization has been our effort in developing the different versions of the program.

SMART-HP (Healthcare professionals): Despite all the phenomenal progress in medical science, the present-day healthcare professionals are the most burnt out they have ever been. Many factors account for the same including the invasion of electronic medical records, the pressures of pay per value, loss of autonomy, excessive regulations, moral distress, and productivity pressures. Healthcare professionals sometimes get cynical when offered stress management and resiliency programs without any credible effort toward changing the workload.

One of the earliest steps in SMART with healthcare professionals is to acknowledge the real need for organizational strategies. It is also important to emphasize that:
- ◊ Organizational strategies take time and are expensive
- ◊ With a fixed and limited budget, there is only so much the leaders can do
- ◊ **Once the burnout sets in, it takes years for the brain changes to reverse**
- ◊ Burnout predisposes to worse quality and higher cost of care, a decline in personal health, professionalism, relationships, and work satisfaction

◊ The purpose of enhancing individual resilience isn't to become passive about organizational issues. On the contrary, it will help you preserve the strength to become a change agent

Organizational (the outside-in) and personal (the inside-out) strategies don't conflict with each other. They are like two wheels of a bicycle, supportive of each other, as shown in the figure below.

Organizational and personal resilience are like two wheels of a bicycle—supportive of each other

SMART shares this perspective in a humble and participatory approach, and then provides the insights and skills with the following in mind:

◊ Integrating science and evidence-base is even more critical for healthcare professionals
◊ Shorter-duration sessions help with participation
◊ Offering skills that help return joy to the practice are more meaningful
◊ Improving relationships in personal life helps one develop an optimal work-life balance
◊ Customization to the subgroups in healthcare is essential

SMART-W (Workforce): Many of the challenges mentioned for healthcare professionals also apply to the non-healthcare workforce. At most workplaces, a combination of organizational and individual approaches offers the best solution. In the corporate world, there is a stigma around stress and anxiety. Personal privacy is thus essential. Avoiding labels and diagnoses thus helps enhance participation.

SMART for workforce adapts to the tremendous diversity that is part of corporate culture. Programs that honor different lifestyles instead of the traditional family unit are more likely to resonate with a broader audience. Engagement of the leadership at the highest level is critical to the long-term success of the program. Connecting resilience to health-related and occupational outcomes is as important as connecting it to lower stress and greater happiness.

SMART-P (Patients): SMART has been adapted to a broad spectrum of diagnoses including mood disorders (particularly anxiety and depression), for patients with cancer, chronic pain, GI conditions, addiction, chest pain, for cardiac rehab, in couples with infertility, in couples with intimacy issues, for pediatric population, and more.

The specific adaptations are too numerous and specific to elaborate here. Some of the particular concepts linked with individual diagnoses are:
- ◊ Depression—Greater focus on validation and self-compassion
- ◊ Anxiety—Greater emphasis on relaxation and acceptance
- ◊ Patients with cancer—Connect resilience with better cancer-related outcomes
- ◊ Chronic pain—Share the concept of total pain (physical + emotional + spiritual) and how resilience can help decrease the total pain; share the neuroscience of central sensitization
- ◊ GI conditions—Recognize the chronicity of symptoms particularly functional GI disorders (such as irritable bowel syndrome), validate the symptoms, nurture acceptance, and provide ways to relax
- ◊ Addiction—Stress is one of the strongest predictors of relapse. SMART is mostly used in relapse prevention strategies by decreasing stress and helps develop better self-control

◊ Chest pain—Emphasize some of the physiology of autonomic nervous system and how the skills can enhance vagal tone, decrease sympathetic activity, and decrease recurrence of chest pain

◊ Cardiac rehab—Share the importance of positive emotions in rehab and how SMART can help participants access these emotions along with improving relationships

◊ In couples with intimacy issues—SMART fosters a deeper connection between the partners that is based on mutual respect and honoring the other person for who they are, instead of focusing primarily on the physical aspects

◊ For children—Several pediatric psychologists, nurses, and physicians have applied SMART among children. We have found that children generally resonate much better with gratitude and compassion, compared to acceptance and meaning. Many of the attention practices also work very well with children.

These are just a few of the conditions for which we have tested the benefit of SMART. In the coming years and decades, I hope to adapt it to most of the major diagnoses. I believe **we can help almost every patient by enhancing their coping and resilience skills** leveraging the concepts and skills of SMART.

SMART-C (Caregivers): Caregivers are the silent patient. They often experience greater stress than the patients themselves. However, their struggles often are not acknowledged and validated. Of all the groups that I have worked with, if there is one group that needs skills in coping and stress management the most, it is the caregivers.

SMART helps caregivers with validating their stresses, find moments where they can have emotional respite, learn ways to reframe, bring meaning in their efforts, and cultivate greater acceptance and forgiveness. Caregivers are empowered to access the much-needed rest so they can continue to serve to their best ability.

SMART-S (Students): Students today are stressed for many reasons some of which are insufficient sleep, academic overload, peer pressure, complicated relationships, lack of exercise, the burden of loans, inadequate housing and excessive time spent online. They also have limited coping skills.

SMART helps students understand their stressors from a neuroscience perspective and provides emotional solutions to reframe their challenges better and helps with real day today struggles like adapting to work overload, dealing with lack of control, helping a stressed-out colleague, and more.

SMART-T (Teachers and other education staff): Although teachers are among the most, if not the most important professionals in our society, they are often under-resourced, overworked, have significant regulatory issues, and have to deal with redundant paperwork. Every teacher also has to act as a mental health professional, caring for students' cognitive as well as emotional needs.

SMART validates the struggles teachers are facing and provides them with skills to redirect their attention toward gratitude and compassion. SMART offers them skills to better work with the difficult students. SMART also provides a way for teachers to connect with other teachers and develop a deeper camaraderie to support each other.

In addition to the above, SMART has been adapted for police chiefs, air force staff, veteran caregivers, and other groups.

I have no doubt we will keep adapting SMART to the needs and preferences of different groups as we expand the scale of the program. From that perspective, I believe, SMART offers an optimal blend of strength and flexibility—strong in its underlying principles, and flexible in its overall approach. This combination of strength and flexibility is what characterizes resilience.

38. SMART Attributes

In developing SMART, we have had the benefit of leveraging research and learnings of thousands of scientists and psychologists and lived experience of hundreds of thousands of learners and patients. We realized that the approach should start with answering why we struggle the way we do from a more in-depth neuroscience perspective. We figured the practices should be short and powerful, provide immediate uplifting emotions, and be relationships centric. Further, the program should steer clear of any clichés, use 21st-century language, and be novel and engaging.

We realized that most practitioners who were trying long sitting meditation were struggling with the practice and were mostly mind wandering. Even though meditation can be beneficial for training attention, it is a difficult practice. For this reason, we didn't include meditation as an initial core practice and only brought it as an additional practice in the third module.

Most people who seem like they are meditating are actually mind wandering

SMART Attributes

The SMART attributes I share with you below integrate our learnings over the last fifteen years in developing and refining the program. (Adapted from resiliencetrainer.com).

Ease of Adoption and Practice:

- **Short training time**: The end user can learn the basic program in four 30-minutes sessions or a single two-hour session

- **Novel and engaging**: The concepts and skills are thoughtfully designed to avoid cliché and jargon, are highly engaging, and 'sticky'

- **Integrated approach**: Each practice is only a few seconds to a few minutes long and is embedded in daily routine

- **Relationship-centric**: The skills are designed to enhance relationships with self and others

- **Secular**: The concepts and language are secular and accessible to most

- **Customizable**: The program and skills are customizable to the preferences and constraints of an individual, team, or organization.

- **Quick reward**: The skills provide immediate access to uplifting emotions

Ease of Scalability Across A Broad Spectrum of Scenarios and Audiences:

- **Suited to the workplace**: The program is designed to integrate well within the workplace to help enhance professionalism, engagement, and productivity

- **Highly scalable**: The skills can be taught individually or in groups that range from a few to several hundred

- **Several different models**: Availability in several different models, offering a customizable approach for most individuals and entities

- **College students**: High acceptance by children and college students; pediatric version is in development

- **Broad application**: Offered every year to over 40,000 learners for resilience, wellbeing, and better work performance, and over 5,000 patients and caregivers for better coping and disease modification

Based on Extensive Cutting-Edge Research:

- **Scientifically rooted:** Deeply anchored in science, particularly neurosciences, evolutionary biology, and psychology

- **Research evidence**: Tested and found efficacious in about thirty clinical trials (with high effect size) with about a dozen studies published in peer-reviewed journals, showing promising effectiveness for a breadth of outcomes (stress, resilience, anxiety, mindfulness, wellbeing, happiness, positive health behaviors, burnout, self-reported productivity, and depressive symptoms)
    - An online version of the program found efficacious in three research studies
    - Self-study program found efficacious in a research study

Ready for Broader Dissemination:

- **Train-the-trainer**: A fully-developed train-the-trainer program with over 400 learners trained. A new Certified Resilience Trainer Program recently developed (resiliencetrainer.com)

- **A complete suite of products**: Hundreds of thousands of users have utilized the print, digital, and in-person programs

- **Refined and disseminated** for over a decade after initial development

In designing SMART, we have avoided the following challenges for the end users: Long training duration; significant daily time commitment; difficult practices that are often not fully embedded in daily life; low engagement; high cost; limited scalability; rooted in specific traditions limiting widespread acceptance; ritualistic approaches, limited scientific backing.

39. SMART Sequence

In this final chapter, I wish to provide you with a suggested sequence for progress and also a concise summary of the insight and practices.

The SMART Sequence

(This is an excerpt from my book, *The Resilience Journal*)

I suggest you bring SMART skills to your life in two phases: Train and Sustain.

Train: The Train phase is generally four weeks long (one week for each module) and roughly progresses in the following sequence:

	Week 1	Week 2	Week 3	Week 4
Morning Gratitude	✔	✔	✔	✔
The Two-Minute Rule		✔	✔	✔
Curious Moments		✔	✔	✔
Kind Attention			✔	✔
Resilient Mindset				✔

In other words:
- ◊ Start with morning gratitude for the first week
- ◊ Add the two-minute rule and/or curious moments in the second week

◊   Add kind attention in the third week
◊   Add resilient mindset in the fourth week
◊   From the fifth week onward customize the practices, so they fit well with your lifestyle and preferences

None of this is written in stone. If you find a slightly different way to bring these practices to your life or wish to start with the two-minute rule instead of morning gratitude, that will be completely fine.

Sustain: The sustain phase lasts your entire life where you continue to deepen and broaden your skills. You customize the skills to your life and share with others. I will continue to develop and offer additional insights and perspectives to help your progress in your journey into resilience.

SMART Table
The tables below summarize the most important concepts and skills I have shared in this book.

Topic	Insights	Practices
Module 1: Gratitude	The brain struggles with: Focus Fatigue Fear Most of the time, the brain is in its default (distracted) mode, often thinking neutral or negative thoughts. You can pull your brain out of its default mode by developing strong attention.	Morning Gratitude *First thing in the morning, think about five people in your life who mean a lot to you and send them your silent gratitude.* Gratitude Jar *Write grateful notes to yourself and save them in a jar.*

Topic	Insights	Practices
Module 2: Mindful Presence	The brain focuses on what it finds salient (of value). Over time, what was once exciting and attractive loses novelty, and we notice it less. Practicing mindful presence can overcome these tendencies.	Two-Minute Rule *Give two minutes of undivided attention to at least one person each day who deserves that attention but isn't presently getting it.* Curious Moments *Observe what's around you with a deeper sense of curiosity.*

Topic	Insights	Practices
Module 3: Kindness	Because of our ancestral struggles, our brain is wired to quickly judge others and feel suspicious. The more we find others different from us, the greater our amygdala activation, limiting our kindness. The realization that most people are special and struggling can help you be kind.	Kind Attention *Choose to send a silent good wish to as many people as you can during the day.* Drop One *Drop one (or more) unhealthy habit (prolonged sitting, habitual multitasking, or a daily dose of excessive news).* Restful Moments *Add moments of relaxation such as meditation to your day.*

Topic	Insights	Practices
Module 4: **Resilient** **Mindset**	Our mindset depends on our thoughts. Our brain is by design a conflicted organ and struggles with consistently rational thinking. Aligning your thoughts with timeless principles can help you develop a resilient mindset.	<u>Resilience Thinking</u> *Align your day with one or more of the five principles:* *Gratitude, Compassion, Acceptance, Meaning, Forgiveness* <u>Pick One</u> *Pick one (or more) healthy habit (healthy diet, exercise, sleep).* <u>Find inspiration</u> *Live your day feeling inspired **by** someone or **to** do something.*

Epilogue

I am concerned about the world right now. Most human brains live their day carrying a heavier load than they can lift. Most days we are packing twenty bags of sand in a ten-pound sandbag. As a result, we have little time left for deep thinking. Absence of deep thinking takes away values and sprouts greed, fear, and selfishness.

The problem with greed and selfishness is that they win in the short term. Our current state of emotional and spiritual infancy makes many of us myopic—focused on the short term. How did my company perform this quarter?

Presently the world's momentum is toward accelerating speed, greed, fear, and selfishness. Ask yourself these three questions:
Will the internet be faster a year from now or slower?
Will you get more emails a year from now or fewer?
Will you have lesser or more hurts and regrets in a year?

Likely, your cognitive and emotional load will be higher a year from now than it is today. Probably, your capacity to lift the load may be lower a year from now. Hence the need to have a personal plan to make sure your brain keeps pace with the change.

We must take charge of our brain, choose where and to what depth you deploy your attention, and interpret based on your values. While you and I can't change the world (the road), we can change the micro-universe around us (the car) and the brain that sits in our head (the driver). And if we all did that, the world will change.

My friend and colleague, Angie showed a perfect example of personal transformation. Angie was sitting by the side of her nephew who lay on a gurney with a self-inflicted gunshot wound to his head. Angie was distraught, angry, sad.

Then she remembered that it was Tuesday, the day of compassion. Angie changed her reaction to compassion. She sent compassion to her nephew, and also to his parents, the medical team, and everyone around her. She became a healer at that moment. Despite the tremendous pain, Angie truly embodied a positive energized presence. The loss was irreparable, but she started the path to healing.

Friends, we can't rely on the instinctive brain. We have to take charge and create the brain of our own making. Such a brain will cultivate a strong and intentional focus, and think with the principles of gratitude, compassion, acceptance, meaning, and forgiveness. People owning such a brain will become resilient. Instead of getting crushed by change, they will become a change agent. Instead of blaming "them others," feeling like a victim, and losing locus of control, they will feel empowered to resist oppression. The resulting upward spiral will transform their physical and mental health, relationships, and work.

Just as trees don't make roots the night of the storm, I invite you to start the change today. If you push to tomorrow, you'll push it out by a decade. Start with a small change that you can integrate into your life and persist with it for a few weeks before adding another change.

Here is an email I sent to the participants in the longer Transform course to share a small part of my journey for the last 15+ years.

Title: I hope I am not bragging
Dear friends,

2003:
Someone cuts me off on the road. "Jerk," I mumble beneath my lips. He stays in my head for the next two minutes.

I drive into the parking lot. Someone very attractive, thinly clad, is coming out of her car. My biological instinct is to play a game of genetic roulette with that person. My brain cells fight with each other. I feel guilty.

Walking in the hallway, I see a colleague who I know had given a poor score to my grant application. I force a smile. But deep inside I want an opportunity to review his grant and pay him back in kind. Or at least somehow show him how he was wrong.

I carry a stereotype of who I like. Anyone falling outside that range is detestable. With half the people I see or meet, I carry a Pan-Am smile but am meaning something else inside.

My peace is vulnerable, contingent on freedom from unsatisfied craving or unresolved fear in the past few seconds. I am living a fake, double-faced life. People think I am a good person. I indeed am from the outside. But inside I am shortchanging myself. I feel unhappy, sometimes jealous, angry, frustrated and stressed.

I know I want to be different, feel different, but have no idea how to get there.

I feel sorry for the poor me I was in 2003.

2019:
Someone cuts me off on the road. First instinct—wish them well. I hope he is okay, not in an emergency, and reaches home safely.

Someone attractive crosses my path. First instinct—wish her well. See the other person as a being, not a physical object.

In the hallway run into someone who I know badmouthed me. First instinct—wish him well. I'm sure he knew something I don't know about myself. All I can do is to strive to improve who I am. Hopefully someday he will perceive my kindness.

The result: I am more flexible, love to meet people, feel good about myself, and mostly am in a hopeful cheerful disposition. No double face, minimal judgment, and consistency between inner thought process and external behavior. There is more time to pay attention to the seasons, watch little kids grow, and just "be."

What a journey it has been...the last fifteen years!

I am grateful to you for walking along.

I wish we could bring the whole world with us! Don't you?

I am grateful to you for staying with me through this book and hope we get to connect in life. I am and always will be a work in progress. But I promise to you that I strive to live each day of my life with the principles I have shared with you.

I wish you hope, peace, joy, and love.

Amit

Acknowledgements

I am grateful to the countless scientists, reporters, philosophers, and authors who have helped me learn the information I share in this book.

I am grateful to every person who has helped me smile, smiled at my sometimes not-so-funny jokes, and helped me keep a light heart.

I am grateful to my parents, Sahib and Shashi; my in-laws, Vinod and Kusum; my brother, Kishore; my sisters, Sandhya and Rajni; my daughters, Gauri and Sia; and my wife, Richa, for showering me with love that sustains me every day.

I am grateful to all my friends and colleagues for their support and love.

I am grateful to you all for helping build a kinder, happier, and more hopeful world for our planet's children. Thank you.

Amit

About Dr. Sood

Dr. Amit Sood is married to his lovely wife of 25 years, Dr. Richa Sood. They have two girls, Gauri age 14 and Sia age 8.

Dr. Sood serves as the Executive Director of the Global Center for Resiliency and Wellbeing and The GRIT Institute. Dr. Sood is the creator of Mayo Clinic Resilient Mind program and is a former professor of medicine, chair of the Mind-Body Medicine Initiative, and director of student life and wellness at Mayo Clinic.

Dr. Sood completed his residency in internal medicine at the Albert Einstein School of Medicine, an integrative medicine fellowship at the University of Arizona and earned a master's degree in clinical research from Mayo Clinic College of Medicine. He has received several National Institutes of Health grants and foundation awards to test and implement integrative and mind-body approaches within medicine.

Dr. Sood has developed an innovative approach toward mind-body medicine by incorporating concepts from neuroscience, evolutionary biology, resilience, mindfulness, psychology, philosophy, and spirituality. His resulting program, Stress Management and Resiliency Training (SMART©) helps patients learn skills to decrease stress and enhance resiliency by improving self-awareness, engagement, and emotional resilience. Interventions adapted from the program reach approximately 50,000 patients and learners each year. The program has been tested in about 30 clinical trials.

Dr. Sood's programs are offered for a wide variety of patients and learners including to improve resiliency; decrease stress and anxiety; enhance well-being and happiness; cancer symptom relief and prevention;

and wellness solutions for caregivers, corporate executives, health care professionals, parents, and students. SMART© program is now integrated in several hospitals and health systems for managing burnout, leadership training, for enhancing resilience among nurses, and is offered to students and teachers.

Dr. Sood has authored or co-authored over 70 peer-reviewed articles, and several editorials, book chapters, abstracts, and letters. He has developed award-winning patient education DVDs on topics within integrative medicine ranging from paced breathing meditation and mindfulness to wellness solutions for obesity, insomnia, and fibromyalgia. Dr. Sood is the author of the books *The Mayo Clinic Guide to Stress-Free Living, The Mayo Clinic Handbook for Happiness, Immerse: A 52-Week Course in Resilient Living, and Mindfulness Redesigned for the Twenty-First Century.* As an international expert in his field, Dr. Sood's work has been widely cited in the press including—*The Atlantic Monthly, USA Today, Wall Street Journal, New York Times, NPR, Reuters Health, Time Magazine (online), Good Housekeeping, Parenting, Real Simple, Shape, US News, Huffington Post, Mens Health Magazine, The Globe and Mail, CBS News, Fox News, Everyday Health, and others.* He has interviewed with several prominent TV and radio shows, both nationally and internationally. He served as the February 2015 Health care pioneer for the Robert Wood Johnson Foundation.

He is a highly sought-after speaker and delivered the TEDx talk—*Happy Brain: How to Overcome Our Neural Predispositions to Suffering.* He has mentored several hundred fellows, medical students, instructors, consultants, and residents.

Dr. Sood has received several awards for his work, including the Mayo's 2010 Distinguished Service Award, Mayo's 2010 Innovator of the Year Award, Mayo's 2013 outstanding physician-scientist award, and was chosen as one among the top 20 intelligent optimists "helping the world be a better place" by *Ode Magazine.*

Additional Resources

Books: *Mayo Clinic Guide to Stress Free Living*
Mayo Clinic Handbook for Happiness
Immerse: A 52-Week Course in Resilient Living
Mindfulness Redesigned for the Twenty-First Century
Stronger: The Science and Art of Stress Resilience

The Resilience Journal: A 2-Minute Commitment to Lift Your Entire Day
Happier Mornings Calmer Evenings: A Gratitude and Kindness Curriculum

Websites: Resilientoption.com (bounceback.net)
Resiliencetrainer.com (thegritinstitute.org)
Myhappinesspal.com

Social Media: @amitsoodmd

Train-the-trainer course: Transform + Trainer Skills Intensive

Please access resiliencetrainer.com if you are interested in pursuing SMART training or wish to bring SMART to your organization.

Made in USA - Kendallville, IN
61257_9780999552544
01.22.2024 1338